Do
Improvise

Less Push. More Pause. Better Results
A New Approach to Work (and Life)

Robert Poynton

Published by
The Do Book Company 2013
Works in Progress Publishing Ltd
thedobook.co

Text © Robert Poynton 2013
Illustrations © Andy Smith 2013

The right of Robert Poynton to
be identified as author of this
work has been asserted by him in
accordance with the Copyright,
Designs and Patents Act 1988

A CIP catalogue record for this book
is available from the British Library

ISBN 978-1-907974-01-4

3 5 7 9 10 8 6 4

To find out more about our
company, books and authors,
please visit **thedobook.co**
or follow us on Twitter **@dobookco**

5% of our proceeds from the
sale of this book is given to
The Do Lectures to help it achieve
its aim of making positive change
thedolectures.com

Cover designed by James Victore
Book designed and typeset
by Openhouse Creative
Based on series design by Ratiotype

Printed and bound by Livonia Print
on Munken, an FSC-certified paper

Contents

For Beatriz

1
The Promise

I was going to make chicken with olives.

Cooking a traditional Spanish dish would, I felt, be a cunning way to show my new relations how well I was adapting to life in Madrid. But, as often happens, the dinner was postponed. Thursday suited me just as well as Tuesday, or so I thought. However, when I took the ingredients out of the fridge, a pungent smell declared that the chicken was no longer quite the thing to offer to guests.

So I had to improvise.

Into the bin went the chicken, along with my original idea and hopes of looking impressive. Instead I lashed up a boringly simple pasta sauce with onion, tuna and tomato. Yet my guests were impressed. My wife's Aunt Carmen asked what I had done to give it such a spicy tang. I was curious myself because I couldn't remember using anything spicy, so I shrugged it off, hoping to make it look as if there were a secret ingredient that was part of a master plan.

Unless buying the chicken three days too early counts, there was no master plan. However, there *had* been a secret ingredient. So secret not even I knew what it was. Only later did I remember that the previous night, my cast-iron frying pan had played host to some spicy little Spanish peppers called 'pimientos de padron'. It was the oil they had left behind that had given unexpected verve to my pasta sauce.

Cooking is frequently like this. As is life, and work. The unexpected is our constant companion. Blind alleys, unheralded turns and serendipitous connections are everyday stuff. However hard we work to avoid it, we are constantly accosted by things we didn't plan for, from a puncture to a deflating economy. Life is a whirling torrent for which nobody has a script.

Such a complex world demands an improvised response. Even in theory, there could never be a script - all the money and all the computing power in the world could never produce one. Things are far too complex for that. The world, even our little bit of it, changes faster than we can track. Since everything is interconnected, it is unpredictable, and always will be. Our attempts to break it down into manageable pieces are of limited use, because wholes - like families, organisations or people - have properties that don't lie in the parts.

Yet somehow we cope. Prosper even. We succeed in ways we can't imagine and get results we don't expect for reasons we couldn't anticipate. Though we rarely tell the story like that afterwards.

We are, in fact, naturally good at creative adaptation and there is a substantial measure of it in all that we do. We flex, respond, adjust, re-adjust, amend, refine, tailor or tweak what we are doing all the time. In short, like all living things, we are capable improvisers.

So it is odd that we ignore or disparage improvisation. We generally see it as a last resort, or a sign of failure. It is not respectable, particularly for people in positions of power or eminence, to improvise. When we catch them at it, we say, with scorn, that they are 'winging it'.

This is a shame and a waste. By maligning improvisation we lose out on several counts. First, we misunderstand our success. By ignoring how our ability to adapt contributes to our achievements, we waste time and effort. We make (and repeat) errors we could avoid.

Second, we don't develop our improvisational ability any further. We put a ceiling on a capacity that could give us far more than we realise. What little we do use, we use clumsily. We make up for this by working harder and harder at the things that we *do* regard as important, such as planning and analysis, which inevitably deliver diminishing returns. We end up trying to impose control even in areas (such as creativity and innovation) where it *really* isn't appropriate. When that doesn't work we get frustrated and stressed. So we do more of the same, but this time we push harder. Like a gerbil on a wheel, we end up running ever faster and going nowhere.

Thirdly, and somewhat sadly, by ignoring improvisation we also ignore a part of ourselves, misreading our own nature. A great gift becomes an orphaned child that we banish from our sight. As a consequence, something beautiful is lost.

This is a great loss. However, it is also a wonderful opportunity.

The 'offer' here, as an improviser would say, is to learn to understand, trust and develop our ability to improvise. To become both more willing and more adept at flexing, adapting and adjusting to what we have, rather than wishing we had something else. If we do, our lives can become easier and simpler, with more fun and less stress. It provides a way to increase our productivity that doesn't rely on trying harder. To put it more prosaically, we can get more done, more easily. This is quite a prospect.

It is like learning a second language. Becoming fluent in another language enlarges your understanding. You see and hear things that you didn't see or hear before. You can connect with new people in a different way. It enriches how you think. A wealth of possibilities that were closed to you open up.

The promise of becoming a more fluent improviser is similar. It gives you a new dimension. Where before there were only problems, now you see 'offers' as well. Instead of lamenting setbacks you focus on finding a way to use them. When you get stuck, you aren't fazed. You learn to pause because you know that paying close attention is a more fruitful response than madly rushing around. Difficulty doesn't disappear, but you engage with it, instead of struggling *against it.*

Improvisers have developed the ability to create a coherent story, incorporating interruptions, objections and curve balls seamlessly as they go. They are able, constantly, to build ideas and relationships, even in the most demanding circumstances. These are abilities we would all do well to develop.

This means more than polishing a few neglected skills. It represents quite a shift in attitude. Instead of trying to bend events (and people) to your will, you focus on discovering a way to work with whatever you find. This can be very liberating. You realise that you don't have to know everything. That you don't always have to be 'on top of things', that you can allow yourself to be 'in the thick' of them. That you can use physical cues like position or space to cut through clever talk and create real action. That a simple shift from 'yes, but' to 'yes, and' can make you far more creative. There are, in fact, plenty of sensible, intelligent and practical ways of behaving, many of which you already do, that don't require command or control. At heart this attitude is founded on humility and acceptance, which helps you to become more compassionate, especially to yourself. It is a lighter way of being.

Improvisational ability isn't a special talent you are born with (or without) but something we all have in some measure that can be practised and developed. The aim of this book is to give you some ideas about how to do that and show you why it is worth the effort. Namely, that improvising well enables you to use the resources you have in a more satisfying, surprising and enjoyable way.

Learning this new 'language' does not imply abandoning the old one, any more than learning Chinese implies forgetting your English. The aim is not to have one supplant the other but to broaden your repertoire and give you a new resource to work with. It is a complementary approach, not an alternative one. As an improviser would put it, it is a 'Yes, and ...' Of which more later.

People think of improvisation as unruly and chaotic but, in fact, it is a discipline with a system of rules that guide your conduct. This improvisational discipline has a number of uncommon virtues. It assumes that events around you, and the people that provoke most of those events, are beyond your control. As a result it discourages you from wasting any time or energy trying, in vain, to control them. Instead, it focuses on how to use whatever they give you, even if it is a challenge or an objection, and trains you to see these as opportunities. It pays attention to what you *can* control, which is your own attitude and response to whatever happens. This seems very wise to me. Ultimately, the primary struggle that each of us face in life is with ourselves anyway.

The essence of the method can be captured in a small number of practices. By practices I mean simple habits which act as guiding ideas in any situation and shape (but do not dictate) your response. Thus, although this is, like any book, just words on a page, it is a book about doing, and the ideas explained here really start to deliver once you start to use them, to put them into practice in your own way, for your own purposes.

You can plug these practices directly into everyday life. There are plenty of opportunities to do so. An infinite number, in fact. At any moment, when stuck, or floundering, or in search of something new or different, the practice of improvisation offers you simple questions that will provoke action (like 'how can I see this difficulty as something to use?') It can be applied to almost anything.

However, for some people, this might mean that there are too many opportunities. With so much choice, you can become paralysed. So I have given you another way in, which is to start with a few games. After each chapter I have chosen a 'killer' game that brings to life some of the ideas explained in that chapter. There is an explanation of how to set up, run and debrief each one.

This gives you something concrete to try. Improvisational exercises have clear and simple rules, which gives them structure. They have a limited duration (most of them only take a few minutes). They can be used for a specific purpose - like generating new ideas. All in all they provide a very tangible introduction to the practices.

Each of these games are tried and tested but they can

be used in many different ways. They are exercises my colleagues and I have used hundreds of times to create powerful learning experiences for all sorts of different groups. I have included some ideas about what we have used them for - though I am sure that you will find ways to use them that I haven't thought of.

Even the simplest games have a lot packed into them, so it still takes quite a few words to explain them.

Since improvisation deals with the fundamentals of how people interact it can be applied very widely to everything from personal relationships to spiritual awareness. Nonetheless, in the pages that follow we are going to concentrate on three particular themes that are important to our organisations as well as ourselves, namely: communication, creativity and leadership.

Whatever the area you are interested in, improvisational practice offers you a way to act yourself into a new way of thinking (rather than think yourself into a new way of acting). By encouraging you to act differently, it creates the space for you to think differently. By engaging the whole person - body and soul - it short-circuits our cleverness and stops us thinking ourselves into a corner. It is also very simple. The main ideas can be explained in a single chapter, which is the one coming up. Take that on board and you can immediately set off on your very own inquiry. The downside is that you need to be willing to be playful and have fun along the way. But that is just a price you have to pay.

2
The Practice

The practices of improvisation are very obvious. There is nothing unique or special about them. This is not, as the saying goes, rocket science. It is more like making a paper aeroplane - with a little instruction everyone can do it. You can then have endless fun experimenting with your own variations.

This may disappoint you - complex solutions often feel impressive, even seductive. But once you get over your disappointment, I am sure it will be a relief to realise that you won't have to grapple with pages of equations, just make a few folds in a sheet of paper, as it were.

The improv practices are not radically novel, indeed they may well feel familiar. However, I make no apology for this, because in my view, originality is over-rated. With rare exceptions, the most powerful new ideas are combinations of old ones, re-expressed.

What you will find here falls into that category. It is both simple and obvious, which I think is a good thing. The benefits of simplicity are obvious. And the benefits of being obvious are quite simple - you don't have to work so hard.

The combination of the two means that the practices of improvisation can be understood quickly and easily. There is subtlety here too, but the essentials can be covered in a single chapter. Give me twenty minutes and you will be out of here, having learned something you can use for the rest of your life.

This is a big claim, but I am happy to make it because I know it to be true. People say things like, 'Four and a half years ago I was in a session of yours and I still remember what you said about offers ...' This is amazing, but in fact it occurs quite regularly. Quite a contrast to my home life, where no one can remember anything I said four and a half minutes ago.

One of the most beautiful things about working with these ideas is to see how a seemingly small shift can make such a big difference. Simple and obvious it may be. Trivial it isn't.

The practice can be summed up in six words. They are: Notice More, Let Go, Use Everything. You see, I told you we could do this quickly. Now that you have the basics you can start to use them. Let's try right here, right now, as you read this book.

How could you '*notice more*'? Perhaps, as you read, you could observe your own feelings as they arise in response to my words. When are you curious, engaged or puzzled? Notice that and you might learn something about yourself as well as about these ideas.

You could '*let go*' of an expectation - that improvisation is frivolous, for example. Doing that would help you to appreciate how, in fact, we are all always improvising, and to discover how that ability is critical to leadership.

You might '*use everything*' by trying to explain something you are struggling with to somebody else. Doing so will clarify your understanding. Moreover, there is a good chance that the other person will give you a new way of looking at it. Even if they don't, by asking their opinion, you have given them a little gift. You have used your struggle to build a relationship. Nice move.

This goes on for ever. With presence of mind, you can apply these ideas at any moment, in any context. You will always have new opportunities to notice more, let go and use whatever is happening. At home, at work and at play. As often as you like, with whoever you like. It is a promiscuous practice.

Nonetheless, it acts as a discipline. You just keep asking the same questions and the circumstances create plenty of novelty. You don't need to keep learning new things, you just practise familiar ones which turn out to be endlessly useful. This is highly economical. With practice, things become easier and, as golfers say, the more you practise the luckier you get.

In a way, it is even simpler still, because, as you may have noticed, the three main ideas are interconnected. Let me demonstrate, using the examples I gave above.

Noticing your feelings (*notice more*) gives you something else to use (*use everything*).

Letting go of an expectation frees you up to notice more of what I am saying.

Trying to use *everything*, even the bits you don't like, encourages you to let go of labels.

And so on. Each one naturally gives rise to the other. Which means it doesn't matter where you start.

Remembering six words is unlikely to test your memory. However, just in case, let me suggest a single, keystone expression that we can hang the whole thing on.

It is (cue drum roll): 'Everything's An Offer'.

'Everything's An Offer' lies in the sweet spot. It falls at the intersection of 'Notice More', 'Let Go' and 'Use Everything'. Here's why.

To see everything as an offer means to regard *everything* that occurs as something you can *use*. To do that, you need to really *notice* what's there, not just cruise through life thinking about lunch. In turn, this means *letting go* of labels, knee-jerk responses or conventions. There it is - all three ideas are packed in. They come together as a coherent body of knowledge, which, just like a physical body, has distinct parts that hang together as a unit.

This not only saves us a whole three words but makes the practice ripe for summing up, in time-honoured fashion, as a TLA (three-letter acronym). Namely, EAO. Now we're down to three letters.

However, before we get too excited about this contraction we should bear in mind Einstein's observation that 'everything should be as simple as it can be, but no simpler'. So, let's take a few minutes to look at each of these ideas in turn. There is nothing wrong with taking things to pieces as long as you remember that they are also connected.

Notice More

Normally, we don't notice very much. Certainly not in relation to the amount of information that is bombarding us, every second of every day. In fact, our senses don't just gather information, they play an active role in screening much of it out. For example, the cells in the retina of the eye are arranged so that some signals are passed on while others are ignored.

Much of this selection is automatic. It happens

unconsciously and effortlessly. We are primed to give our full attention to things like fast-approaching cars and crying children, but most things tend to gently fade into the background, particularly if they aren't changing much.

This makes sense. With too much information out there we need ways to economise, to narrow things down. It is as if we have a kind of cerebral screen-saver that automatically kicks in, unless something juicy (like danger, food or sex) crops up.

Happily, our conscious choices make a difference. We can override the automatic processes and choose what we pay attention to. However, this requires effort, as any school teacher (or pupil) knows only too well.

Given this, simply saying to ourselves we should try harder to '*notice more*' isn't going to get us very far. We need some more specific things to do to help us establish the practice.

There are four broad categories where there is more to notice - the wider world, the immediate environment, other people and yourself. That should just about cover it, though if you are able to notice what you are noticing as well, that is a plus (this will give you some insight into yourself and tell you where you could make more effort).

A good place to start is to 'lean into your senses'. Often we get wrapped up with what is going on inside our heads and don't really look, or listen. The challenge here is to get out of your head (as it were). Look at something as if you were trying to draw it. If it's a rose or a Ferrari you may leap from what you already know of such things and assume it is red, without really looking. It is really? Or do parts of it, from the angle you look, appear nearer black? Is it the same red all over? Focus on the sensation, not the label. If a colleague (or partner) launches into a familiar speech, do you leap ahead and start to think of what you want to say next? Can you slow down, and listen to the words they actually say, not the ones you expect? Can you hear the intonation and the qualities of their voice as well? Can you listen for the pauses, for what they are *not* saying, for where the emotion lies, for how the rhythm varies? Can you listen to them as if you were going to repeat every word they said, echoing how they said it?

Another approach is via the idea of opening up, rather than leaning into, your senses. Can you include things that are on the edge? Can you learn to love the corner of your eye? Sit at your desk and listen. Can you let more in, instead of filtering stuff out? Can you hear the air conditioning, the clock, the hubbub of voices, the photocopier, an aeroplane overhead, and still hear your own breathing? Can you take this kind of listening into a conversation?

Or, to open up the analogy itself, can you stretch your listening to include people you don't normally notice? Can you hear new, different or dissenting voices? Can you really listen to them too?

Adam Morgan, founder of brand consultancy eatbigfish, argues that the challenger brands which create an impact out of proportion to their size do exactly this. They look outside the category they are in to find ideas and inspiration in areas that their competitors don't even notice. They might be in insurance but they look at what is happening in the world of coffee or underwear and use what they notice to build their business.

Another way to notice more is to make sure you are using all of your senses. We are primarily visual so sight can easily dominate. Play around with that. If you want to listen better, try closing your eyes. You might not dare to do that in a meeting, but practise while you are listening

to music and you can develop the ability to listen more deeply even with your eyes open.

Make sure you aren't abandoning whole senses. In the countryside, scent announces the opening of flowers, the onset of rain, the ripening of fruit, the proximity of water. Exhaust fumes and fast food aren't quite so attractive so in a city we tend to close down our sense of smell altogether. Reactivate it. You might want to start in a coffee shop or a bakery, where the sensation is going to be more pleasant, but see if you can develop a willingness to notice the ways things smell and the ideas and emotions that are sparked off as a result.

Notice more about your own body. It is more than a means of transport. It houses your mind, which, isn't simply located in your head (for example, neurotransmitters that affect how we think are secreted throughout the body, particularly in the gut). Neuroscientist Candace Pert uses the word 'bodymind' and refuses to use either 'body' or 'mind' separately, to show how overlapping the two really are.

Instead of getting lost in your thoughts, notice your posture, your breathing. Where do you hold tension (the jaw? the neck?) A skilful reading of your own body will not only tell you when you are tense but, for example, when to speak up and when to sit back, or whether the person across from you needs reassurance or encouragement and so on. This gives you a whole new source of information that will help you make decisions or have ideas.

Pay attention to the qualities of things. If your eye is taken by someone in the street who looks beautiful to you (or ugly, for that matter), see if you can notice what it is about them that makes you feel that. Is it the symmetry of their face, the grace of their gait, the line of the jaw? What is it that you are actually seeing when you think 'they are beautiful'?

These are all ways of training yourself to become a more active participant in what you observe. You can't notice everything. Nor would you want to, but what you can do is learn to become more conscious, more active and more discerning. You can deepen your capacity to be present to the world and, most importantly, to the people around you. Do so and you will find new possibilities and opportunities you never expected. In a sense, awareness is all. We should use it wisely.

Let Go

Letting go sounds dangerous. From childhood onwards we are told to hold on. Hold on to Mummy's hand, hold on while the train is moving, hold on to that job. The idea that we should jettison or abandon things goes against the grain.

What, then, does it mean, to 'let go'? What is it we need to let go of, and why?

The short answer is that we need to let go of baggage from the past and extrapolations into the future, because they stop us paying proper attention to the present, and the present is where we live.

I see this very clearly in workshops. People are quick to judge that what we are going to do is silly or that they won't be able to do it. They arrive at a conclusion immediately. The same happens in everyday life. We instantly conclude that John is dull or that his idea is a bad one without pausing to even take it in. This tendency is exacerbated by 'the Facebook effect'. Technology encourages us to rate everything immediately in a simplistic way. These mental short-cuts turn into pre-judgements, or 'prejudice'.

This makes life perversely difficult. You cannot adapt to what unfolds if you aren't even properly aware of it. If you instantly decide how things are, you give them no chance to become anything else. You allow yourself little room for manoeuvre and few options, which makes you tense or nervous. Your chances of responding in a way that is fitting or fresh are remote.

This can be hard to see, not just because such snap judgements come so readily, but because they tend to be self-fulfilling, especially when it comes to judging ourselves. 'You see,' someone will say to me after a game, 'I told you I couldn't do this.' But they have made the experience fit their interpretation, not the other way round. At the cost of their own performance, they have made themselves right - and we do so enjoy being right.

This is why it is important to resist the knee-jerk reaction to leap to conclusions. This doesn't mean forgetting everything you know but it does mean actively letting go of presumptions. Past experience is important, but it can imprison us. Instantly evaluating what is happening through the lens of the past, either while it's going on or before it even happens, gives you no chance of adapting creatively.

In this respect your mind is like your basement. Stuff has a natural tendency to pile up. If you don't keep clearing it out, it becomes uselessly clogged. You don't have to trash the lot but if you don't keep letting stuff go, it soon piles up again.

The other place our minds readily escape to is the future. We are as quick to generate expectations as we are to leap to conclusions. In many ways this is very helpful, because it enables us to act even when we don't have much information. However, it can also trip us up.

Imagine Malcolm and Duncan acting out a scene. Malcolm mentions his pet 'Fido'. Duncan immediately infers this is a dog and acts accordingly, talking about leads, bones and other doggy things, failing to notice that Malcolm went on to say it was a goldfish. Duncan looks like an idiot, Malcolm feels exposed, neither of them know what to do and the audience sees two people who aren't working together at all, which they hate.

Improvisers call this kind of expectation a shadow story. It is not the actual story, but a 'shadow' of that story projected forward into the future, which (just like a snap judgement) prevents us from paying attention to what is actually happening. This becomes a serious problem when, like Duncan, we try to impose our imagined future on the reality. When we do that, the flow of ideas, the relationship between us and the impression we give to anyone looking on all suffer.

Once again, the trouble is that we do this very readily.

It isn't something that only happens on stage. We see someone look at their watch and assume they are getting impatient, from which we infer that they have no interest in our ideas, or for that matter in us at all, and they never have; in fact it is pretty clear that they regard us as incompetent time-wasters. We'll show them, we decide, without bothering to check any of our assumptions, and decide to go on the attack, give them the cold shoulder, or pour scorn on any idea they might have the audacity to suggest. We generate this shadow story in a matter of seconds and all because they looked at their watch.

What we need to do is let go of the shadow story. You can't stop shadow stories forming, so you have to recognise them for what they are and let them go. As soon as you let go of one another will come along just behind it, so there is plenty of opportunity to practise. Don't try to stop them coming along; all you have to do is open up a little space for the present moment by letting them go. That will make all the difference.

Use Everything

If you can use everything as an offer, there must be plenty of offers out there. Indeed there are. An infinite number, in fact.

The all-encompassing nature of this idea is one of its strengths. It very deliberately supposes that whatever you face, regardless of how inviting or irksome it may seem, is usable in some way. This denies you any wriggle room and forces you to look harder, which is the point. This is what makes it a rigorous and disciplined practice.

Nonetheless, it is useful to acknowledge the variety of what is available. Otherwise you might ignore or dismiss categories that turn out to have very rich pickings.

Let's start with you. You may be glad to know that all your errors and mistakes qualify as offers. This is an incredibly powerful and positive re-framing.

If you see mistakes as offers you learn fast. You may learn how *not* to do something, or use the experience to understand why something didn't work. You might also discover something you weren't looking for, which is how many of the most important discoveries get made. You can see a mistake as a 'mis-take', like an actor on a film set, and regard it as another take, or attempt, in an iterative process that strives to get better.

This doesn't mean you should make mistakes on purpose, but given that they are going to occur anyway, it provides a constructive way to respond and a good way to direct your energy. If mistakes are opportunities, you don't need to make apologies, look for scapegoats or find excuses: you just get on with working out how to use them. If you have a glue that fails to stick permanently you might invent the Post-It note.

My colleague Gary once lost his glasses on the way to a workshop and used it to create real intimacy with the group he was working with - he had to get everyone really close so he could see them.

There is no situation too bleak to be reframed in this way. Misfortune, as well as mistakes, can also be regarded as offers. Zen master Suzuki Roshi was in hospital with suspected hepatitis. When this turned out to be cancer, what he saw was the chance to share food with his visitors (because, unlike hepatitis, cancer isn't contagious). It takes great strength to meet such adversity with this kind of fortitude, and it didn't alter the fact he had cancer, which sadly he ultimately died from. However, a heartfelt commitment to look for offers can be a source of such strength for oneself, and of inspiration to others, as it was with Suzuki.

Other people are a constant source of offers. They always bring interpretations, experience and perspective that you don't have. What is obvious to them isn't obvious to you. This is the simple virtue of being obvious that I mentioned at the beginning of this chapter. We often try to be clever or original, when contributing what might seem obvious to us would be more help. You don't have to work as hard as you might think.

When you feel stuck, look for offers from other people. They will provide all manner of fodder for your process, whether they mean to or not. Indeed, even the people who we feel impede or reject our ideas provide a raft of offers, though we might have to work a bit harder to see them.

There is an improv game where a storyteller is given words that have nothing to do with the story she is telling. The word-giver is invited to be as obstructive and awkward as possible. Nonetheless, almost every storyteller ends up finding the words a help, despite the fact they are intended as obstacles. This is because the rules of the game force you to regard them as offers. (You can find out how to play this game at the end of Chapter 5.)

You can apply the same rules outside the workshop. If someone says 'no', you can see it as a request for more information. Or as a test for your ideas. Or you could look for a way to associate, include or connect their objection, which will change your idea, and strengthen it, maybe even improve it. If someone sees things differently from you, instead of thinking they are wrong, see it as an offer. Ask yourself how their point of view can enrich yours.

Can you see what isn't there? In a famous story, Sherlock Holmes brilliantly uses the fact that the dog didn't bark in the night to solve a crime. Ingvar Kamprad, founder of IKEA, once stood in a huge Chinese poultry market, surrounded by thousands of plucked chickens, and asked, 'What do they do with all the feathers?' He saw what wasn't there as an offer, which IKEA then used as a source of filling for bedding. Ask yourself what is missing or absent and see how you could use that too.

Resources are something that are normally missing. We always have less than we would like. You can use shortages to spur your ingenuity. When Robert Rodriguez made *El Mariachi* he didn't have any proper lighting. He used that to make the movie 'moody'. He set it in a small town in Mexico and made a guitar case crucial to the story, because that was all he had. If you want to use what you have, an obvious and easy place to start is simply to ask yourself, 'What have I got?' You might be surprised at how much you have overlooked.

Another group of potential offers is failures and breakdowns. If the projector fails, use it as a chance to have a conversation. Or to create simple, hand-drawn visuals. Or to get people to talk to each other instead of listen to you.

Unforeseen consequences, accidents, acts of god, disasters and delays can all be used to your advantage, if you are prepared to consider them as offers. I have colleagues who have found value in getting on the wrong plane or having their car crushed during a workshop. That doesn't make these good things. But it does stop you thinking of them as bad things. In other words, thinking in terms of using everything reminds you to let go of judgement. You see, it all fits.

I began by saying that the practice is simple. But that doesn't make it easy. Simple and easy are not the same thing at all. The rules of chess are simple enough to be explained in a few minutes. But chess isn't easy.

If you want to use these practices to learn and grow you have to be willing to be changed. Most of us, for understandable reasons, find that tricky. I know this because I have seen it so often. Well-meaning, intelligent, motivated people, who have enthusiastically committed to 'out of the box' thinking, will very often, after an hour or two, be asking for their box back.

Moreover, improvisational practice challenges beliefs that are woven into the very fabric of our thought. Let me give you an example. When we want to understand something, we automatically take it to pieces. We explain bigger things in terms of smaller things. This tendency has driven most of our scientific inquiry for hundreds of years, up to and including the present day.

Yet the (70kg) person you love most in the world is more than 43kg of oxygen, 16kg of carbon, 7kg of hydrogen, 3kg of nitrogen and so on (they also include a tiny amount of gold, but nowhere near enough to make them as precious as they are to you). Who somebody is, is not the same as what they are composed of. How things are arranged matters a lot.

This may seem obvious, but every day we do things that are just as absurd as breaking down a person into chemical elements. We study people's personalities by analysing their answers to a questionnaire and using clever maths to identify components of personality. Which is still a way of trying to explain who somebody is by breaking them down into pieces. We try to compose high-performing teams by putting the right 'elements' together, as if people were chemicals. We demand strategies that are 'future proof'. We set 'deliverables' for a creativity course.

The invisibility of such assumptions means that ways of thinking which challenge them just seem plain wrong. Our education is lopsided. Years of formal and informal schooling would have us believe that the certain, rational, objective knowledge is the only kind.

Improvisational practice challenges this view. For example, it says that you don't deal with something complex by trying to break it down into pieces. It suggests that our enthusiasm for measurement, analysis and prediction is misguided, and that these activities are often pointless. It suggests that trying to control what happens is neither possible nor desirable. Do you feel challenged yet?

The practice asks something different of you. It encourages you to engage as a whole person, not just a rational mind, in an intuitive way. It welcomes all of you to the game. It recognises and values information that is gathered via feel, bodily sensation, posture and movement. It values speed, responsiveness and fit, over accuracy, precision or regularity. It gives precedence to creating a

flow of ideas and energy rather than arriving at answers. It is a living example of the scientific insight that very simple behaviour (or rules) can generate great complexity.

It selects ideas and actions through evolution rather than evaluation. It demonstrates that we can exert influence and impart direction without control. It emphasises practice over theory and action over conclusions.

Be aware, however, that it won't tell you what to do. As should be obvious by now, these ideas are general, universal even. They are more like a compass than a map. A compass shows you which way is north, but you must observe the terrain for yourself.

This leaves room for you. Indeed, it requires that you show up, which isn't as easy as it sounds. Especially when you find yourself questioning long-cherished but unconscious beliefs. Not once, but again and again.

I think you will find it is worth it. Just as this way of working can generate seemingly magical creations in the improv theatre, it can help each of us, individually and collectively, live more rewarding, creative and sustainable lives, and create more valuable and sustainable organisations.

If you want to know how, read on.

ABOUT THE GAMES

Often, when you introduce improvisational games, you may be met with some resistance and become worried about what to do if people are reluctant to play at all - even if it's just you and a couple of colleagues. I know I was initially. I once asked a wise old friend, 'What do I do if it doesn't work, if they don't want to play?' His response was very wise. 'Would that be it not working?' he asked. 'Or would that be it working in a different way than you expected?'

If people really don't want to participate you could use that (as an offer) to explore why there was such resistance, which might be exactly the conversation they need to have. Other strategems would be to point out the value of play as a means of engaging with uncertainty (not knowing how it ends being an intrinsic part of a game). Or emphasise the value of physically energising a group.

It can also be very persuasive simply to acknowledge that some apprehension or reluctance is entirely natural. People like to be right, so by showing that you understand they are reluctant, you can help them become less so.

GAME

PRESENTS

This is a gift-giving game.

At a glance	Two people give imaginary presents to each other.
Purpose	To show the power of accepting offers, to generate a positive climate.
Mechanics	Everyone plays simultaneously in pairs.
Set-up	Demonstration - one person mimes giving a gift, the other thanks them, unwraps it, says what it is.
Debrief	Ask what people got. Explore how connections were made, how each person contributed.

HOW THE GAME WORKS

This is a game to play in pairs. Let's imagine you and I are going to play together.

I mime picking up a present, turn to you and say, 'I have brought you a present.' My gesture tells you something about the shape, size and weight of the present (round or square, large or small, heavy or light, etc.) This is all I do. It isn't my job to decide what the present is.

You mime taking the present. It is important that you take it as given - for example, you don't take a nice big present instead of the puny little one I offered. You thank me, mime unwrapping the gift and then say what it is. 'Lovely, a ball.' It should be something that fits the size and shape of the gesture I made. The more fitting it is with the gesture, the better. Obvious is good.

To set the game up, walk people through a demonstration with a partner. If you don't have a partner that knows the game get a volunteer to give you the present and direct them as they go. The important bit is saying what the gift is, and if they give the present you can demonstrate that yourself.

Once you have explained it, get people in pairs, and let them give gifts back and forth to each other for a few minutes. Check that people don't stop after one gift, thinking they are done - there is no need to be mean, the presents don't cost anything! They should exchange a good number of gifts before you call them to a halt.

THINGS TO WATCH OUT FOR

In this game you want to encourage people to discover what the gift is in the moment, not to plan ahead. The person giving the present needs to 'let go' of any prior idea of what it is. The person receiving must also let go of any expectation they have and say something which respects the size and shape of the gesture. If it fits in the palm of your hand it could be a ping-pong ball, but not an S-Class Mercedes-Benz (unless it's a toy). Encourage those that receive to come up with simple, obvious things. Tell them that trying to be clever or funny gets in the way.

DEBRIEF

As with any game, the best way to start the debrief is to ask the obvious question, which in this case is 'What did you get?' See what different presents there are. If it is appropriate, call attention to the need to 'notice more, let go and use everything'.

You can point out the positive energy that the game generates, which is normally incredibly clear in the energy and body language. After all, we like getting gifts, even imaginary ones. You could use that to inquire about how this kind of physical energy compares to energy levels in the workplace and what you might do to get similar levels of engagement. You can explore what difference the kind of gesture made. Is it easier if the gesture is precise, or vague? There are parallels with work again - you can ask about the effect it has on other people if the offers we make are very specific, or quite vague. When might each be useful?

People sometimes feel frustrated when giving the gift because the other person didn't 'get it right'. The way the game is set up, there is no 'right', yet often people can't help decide what they want the gift to be and get irritated if the other person doesn't 'get it'. This shows up how much we like to try and control other people and can open the door to a very rich conversation about leadership or communication.

WHEN TO USE PRESENTS

You can use this game simply to make people feel good, to put a little bit of the positive energy, that improvisers call 'fit and well', into the room. Or to introduce the idea of offers, or to talk about accepting, or creating flow, or narrative and story, or the power of incompleteness, or the value of the obvious and so on.

It demonstrates all the basic practices of noticing more (the details of the gesture), letting go (any preconceived ideas of what the present is) and using everything (you take what you are given and make something of it).

EXTENDED VERSION - PRESENTS INTO SCENES

If people get on well with the basic version, there is an extended version you can follow up with. You start in exactly the same way, by giving a gift. Then you just add to that by using the gift to start a little scene. The invitation is to keep the story going for as long as possible. Each person can contribute offers as they see fit.

It helps if you direct people to do something with the present, rather than talking about doing something. Ideally something obvious - for example, if the gift is a golf club, hit a ball. Which might then break a window, lead to an argument with a neighbour, and so on ...

If people get stuck or crash, they can let that story go and start with another gift. That is the escape hatch. But encourage people not to abandon things too quickly. Invite them to play slowly, to allow themselves a few seconds of grace to respond. Encourage them to commit to a gesture or movement without feeling they have to say something immediately. Urge them to tolerate the uncertainty the game brings. Without this coaching, people can be incredibly judgemental and decide they have failed immediately (something we often do in other contexts). With a little help, they often surprise themselves and keep a single story going for a few minutes. Which is no mean feat. If you are playing with a room full of people you can allow different pairs' stories to collide into each other (a dog brings back someone's ball and, hey presto, two gifts are connected).

This extended version allows you to delve into a further range of themes, such as:

— what it takes to stay in flow
— our tendency to judge ourselves and others very quickly
— the effect of different kinds of offers
— where responsibility lies for the story
— what happens if only one person makes offers
— when blocking occurs
— what makes a good story
— what conditions are required for co-creation ... and so on.

There is a lot in this game. It is a gift.

PRESENTS WITH CHARACTERS

It is amazing how much mileage you can get out of a simple game. I have been playing Presents for about 15 years, but during the writing of this book a completely new version popped up.

In this case the new bit is simply to add characters to Presents. Before you start, get suggestions from the group for a relationship - brother/sister, teacher/pupil, that kind of thing. Then each person adopts one of the characters as they give and receive the gift. People can either decide in advance who plays which role, or let that emerge through the action (which is more interesting and only slightly more difficult).

I tried this with a group of people from the 'Do Lectures' (see www.dolectures.com). We chose the relationship prisoner/prison guard. Having these characters to play with made it incredibly easy to build a story. Which leads to a new question about how you might apply this: where would adding characters help you build a story more quickly? Would thinking about the character of your company and your competitors help you to more easily develop strategy, for example?

In the improv community you are expected to acknowledge who you learned a game from. This doesn't necessarily mean that person authored the game, but it is a way of respecting the people you have learned from. The original version of 'Presents' Gary learned from Keith Johnstone and the adaptations here are ones we have developed ourselves at On Your Feet.

3
Communication

Communication is what you do all day. And improvisation is the way you do it.

All day long you are constantly communicating with and responding to other people - in person, on the phone or online. Everything, from a chat in the café to a formal, high-stakes negotiation, passing through emails, meetings, presentations and conference calls, is communication. If you are any kind of leader or executive, communication is what you get paid for. It is what you do with friends. It is what makes your marriage work (or not). It is how you bring up your kids.

Communication is a complex, social, improvisational dance. We are more than postmen, delivering sealed messages. We are the messages. As we communicate we exchange and relate not just factual information, but emotion, identity and desire.

You constantly sense what is being said, on many levels. You adjust what you say and how you say it as a result, ceaselessly, and almost without thinking. However structured the conversation, most of the words you say are chosen spontaneously. You delicately vary tone, inflection, rhythm and volume in response to what others say. Depending on the medium you are using, you will also use gesture, position, posture and facial expression.

When we communicate well it is a great source of satisfaction, even joy. An improv troupe is an extreme example of this, but it doesn't only happen on stage. In all sorts of contexts, it is through communication that we make sense of things, build ideas and create value. We feel connected and appreciated. Good communication is central to our effectiveness and our happiness.

Conversely, when we don't communicate well it is a source of frustration, confusion and anxiety. 'Bad communication' is the single biggest complaint in every organisation I have ever worked with, without exception.

This isn't surprising. Communication is not only important, it is incredibly complex. As well as all the qualities that I mentioned above (of tone, etc.) it also depends upon context, timing, sequence, atmosphere, media, setting and, above all, audience. Communication is, by its very nature, multi-layered. There is so much going on, and so much opportunity for misunderstanding, that in a way it is amazing that people ever communicate at all.

As social beings, we are naturally adept at communication. However, this gift is also a curse. Communication is so instinctive that how we go about it becomes invisible. We can easily fall into unhelpful patterns or behaviours that are hard to see, let alone change.

This is where the improv practice comes into play.

It offers us a lens through which to look at what is going on when we communicate. It lays bare, in very simple terms, what is going on. It x-rays our conversation. For example, if you look at your meetings through the lens of the improv practices, what do you see? What quality of listening is being shown? Are people really present? Who is willing to be changed? Who is being obstructive or 'blocking'? (If it's you, why is that?) Asking any of these questions will help you understand why you have the kind of meetings you have (whether they are good, bad or indifferent) and do something about it. What improv does is provide a very simple, but universally applicable, set of ideas to help you frame what you are doing and saying.

You don't immediately have to change things. Sometimes, understanding is enough. For example, Kathy, a marketing consultant, was working with a company where she used to be an employee. A former colleague was now her client and she found that things were becoming confusing and frustrating. When she looked at what was going on in terms of how they communicated she realised that the vast majority of her offers were being blocked. Seeing this helped. It enabled her to understand why she was feeling frustrated. However, she went a step further.

She noticed that in her new role as a consultant it was her job to be an 'offer launcher'. Many of her offers were bound to get blocked, but that came with the territory. It was something she just needed to accept. She didn't need to *change* anything. The understanding that looking through the improv lens gave her was enough to make her feel very differently about the situation.

I found something similar with Dominic, a client of ours whose communication I found very confusing. He said 'yes' to everything, yet the conversations we had always felt negative, which was disconcerting. Looking at it in terms of offers, I realised that while he said the word 'yes', the tone and the body language that accompanied it were blocks. As indeed, were the lack of follow-up, action or change on his part. This helped me understand the different layers of communication and make some choices about what to do.

It is most important to apply this lens to your *own* communication - it isn't only about the other guy. For example, if I feel John always says 'no' to my suggestions, I should scrutinise my own behaviour, not just blame him for being negative. What might I be doing (or not doing) that leads to him saying 'no'? Maybe he feels I am blocking him and is just responding in kind? This is very common. Few of us notice the blocks that we ourselves dish out. Try this - listen out for all the times you say 'yes, but ...' (or words to that effect) and try and turn them into 'yes, and ...'. That will raise your awareness of how often you block without realising.

You might also ask yourself who you are really listening to - other people, or your own inner voices? Are you bringing baggage, what improvisers call 'a shadow story', from previous conversations into this one? Are you making clear offers? Do you use the offers people are giving you? Are you more concerned with how you come across, or with what other people say? Asking such questions of yourself is a way to look at yourself through the eyes of other people, which, as we shall see, is absolutely fundamental to good communication.

When I introduced these ideas to my friend Adam Morgan he made an astute observation. He said: 'Improv shows you the basic building blocks of communication and relationships. It gives you a fundamental grammar.' Understanding the building blocks enables you to think about how you construct your communication. This includes much more than the words you say.

Film director David Keating often uses 'the ideas that improv rests upon' to inform his film making. On a film set, pressure is high, time is short, people don't know each other well and there is a very hierarchical form of organisation. For his horror film *Wake Wood*, which was shot mostly on location in rural Ireland, David felt that it was very important that he, the director, was really present for the whole crew.

What he decided to do was to arrive at the location very early every morning. He spent some time, alone, on the set thinking through the day's shooting and by the time the crew arrived, he would be visibly working at his trestle table. Every day, he would set up stall precisely where the bus arrived, so that people could see him.

This action was a powerful piece of communication - part carrot, part stick. The carrot was to make himself accessible to everyone, so they could contribute their ideas and suggestions. Being 'in their faces' like this made it easier for anyone to talk to him. The stick was to show them that unlike some directors he, the leader, was physically present and committed. Implicit was the notion that everyone else better had be too.

So far I have focused on interpersonal communication. I have done so deliberately because, even with all the media we have at our disposal, everyday interaction is still the most widespread and all-pervading form of communication there is. Ignore it and you miss most of the action.

However, there is another important reason for this focus on the interpersonal. It shows us, very clearly, that communication is, at heart, all about connecting people. The word itself, which comes from the same root as 'communion', confirms this. It means to share.

It is my firm belief that all forms of communication are, or want to be, two-way. Communication is more than the transmission of data. For communication to happen there must be an exchange of some kind; a stimulus and a response. Something goes out and something comes back as a result. What comes back may be different from what went out - a speech might elicit cheers, boos, a witty riposte or a vehement counter-argument - but it cannot be entirely one-way traffic or you have no communication.

Much of what is commonly called 'communication' in the marketing and political worlds is, in fact, anything but. It is only one-way. It would be more accurate to describe it as 'propaganda' or 'indoctrination', but that doesn't sound very attractive, so it gets 're-branded' as 'communication'. This sleight of hand confuses things.

At some level, communication, if it is to be worthy of the name, has to be about what happens between people. This is obviously true of personal communication, but it is also true of meetings, presentations, conferences and even mass communication.

For example, great speakers, like Winston Churchill or Barack Obama, make a personal connection with everyone listening. Gifted communicators see and acknowledge their audience, so that they feel included, even if they can't literally talk back. Thus, even in a broadcast to millions, it feels like someone is talking to you.

The opposite is true as well. I once went to a Sting concert here in the Sierra de Gredos, in a stunning, natural outdoor arena in the mountains. In stark contrast to the warm-up band, Sting and his musicians seemed oblivious to the surroundings and the audience. However technically accomplished a performance it may have been, I felt there was no communication and therefore no connection, which in my view made it a hugely disappointing concert.

The failure to appreciate this intrinsically two-way nature of communication accounts for much of what people complain about. In my view, the single biggest problem when giving a presentation is forgetting, ignoring or excluding the audience.

For improvisers forgetting the audience is lethal, so they do all sorts of things to create the connection and keep it open and alive. You can use the same ideas to remain connected to your own audiences. Do so, and you will communicate much better.

Let's look at presentations. Every day, about 30 million people agonise over their Powerpoint slides. Yet in every presentation there are three elements. You, your material and your audience. Of the three, the material is the one that matters least. Yet the vast majority of people focus almost exclusively on the slides. We work with many people on presentation skills and hardly anyone ever thinks in a disciplined way about what the audience needs. It is important to understand why this occurs, and we will get to that, but first let's look at what you can do about it.

Audience Requirements

The crucial thing to remember is that members of an audience have needs of their own that have nothing to do with your agenda. If those needs aren't met, they won't be able to listen to you. If you don't attend to them, they won't listen to you.

This is a big point. Communicating, even when you are giving a presentation, is as much about listening as it is about speaking. Seriously. This is what I mean about it being two-way. You might be the one doing most of the talking, but that doesn't mean you have licence to get wrapped up in yourself. You need to push your attention out to the people you are talking to. You will serve yourself best by serving them.

This is partly about being sensitive to the room. My colleague Gary Hirsch and I once ran a workshop in Thailand where we expected about 40 people. Only six turned up (we were that popular). Nonetheless we spent the first five minutes behaving as if we were talking to a room full of 40 people, because that is what we had prepared. Embarrassingly, it took us a while to realise that with a handful of people, we should have a conversation.

Ridiculous though it sounds, this is remarkably easy to do, so we coined a piece of language to stop us doing it again. We call this 'the whites of the eyes'. This acts as a reminder to consciously check what is needed, once we are physically in the room with the audience and can see 'the whites of their eyes'. This forces you to think about how you are going to make a connection with the audience and stops you drifting off into your own little world.

Based on a few other improv practices we fleshed this idea out more fully to create a tool called the Audience Requirements Grid. You can apply it at any level of scale - for a big presentation, small meeting or even an individual conversation - though it really comes into its own with a sizeable audience.

This is how it works. The main audience needs are listed and alongside each there is a space where you write down what you are going to do to meet that need. It looks like this.

Audience need

Trust the driver; why should they listen to me?

Your action:

Who am I, beyond labels?

Your action:

What is expected of them; what are they going to have to do?

Your action:

What are they going to get as a result of listening?

Your action:

Are they being seen and acknowledged?

Your action:

1. Trust the driver

Trusting the driver is about credibility. The audience wants to know why you, in particular, are worth listening to. You need to give them an idea of what experience or understanding or insight you have that makes you credible on this subject. This doesn't mean you need to be (or pretend to be) an expert. It means you need to show sensitivity to the audience by giving them some reason to trust that you are worth listening to, rather than assuming that you have the right to command their attention.

For example, when using improv with a business audience I will explain my background is in business not the arts. When talking to Spaniards, I might use some Spanish slang that demonstrates I know the country. If you are working with Nike, tell them if you have worked with Nike before, and so on.

2. Who am I (the speaker) beyond labels?

If communication is about creating a connection between people, your audience needs to know something about who you are as a person, beyond labels. You may be Director of Operations, but *who* are you? This is mostly about small details, but those details make a big difference.

The need can often be met very quickly, through something as simple as body language - do you stride out, or amble on? The form of your name you choose is another option - are you 'Rob' or 'Robert Poynton, Associate Fellow of the Said Business School'. You might mention some unexpected personal detail, taste or interest. How you dress obviously has an effect, so think about that in advance. This isn't about being confessional, it is about a humanising touch.

One great way to show who you are is to play with

status. For example, a powerful CEO might play low status by mentioning how his kids were defying him that morning. Coming down from the high-status position of centre stage is a particularly effective way to create a connection. You can do this, quite literally, by abandoning the podium. I will sometimes start a workshop sitting on the floor, which elevates the audience, who are sitting on chairs, making them feel important. (I will expand on this idea in Chapter 5 on Leadership.)

As you can see, there are many different ways to do this. I often explain how Gary and I began On Your Feet (we met to talk about a T shirt design, but got waylaid, very productively, by the subject of improv). You could tell a story, or make an observation or ask a question, but one way or another, to give the audience an idea of who you are, it has to be personal.

3. What is expected of the audience; what are they going to have to do?

This is one people normally don't think of. After all, it seems self-evident that the audience is there to listen. Maybe, but even if they are a captive audience you shouldn't assume they are willing to listen. That is their choice.

In fact, there is normally something more you want an audience to do. You might want them to listen in a particular way or listen out for certain things. You might want them to answer some questions, or come up with questions for you, or give you feedback, or report back to someone else, or take part in an exercise, or participate in a reflective conversation afterwards. Whatever it is, let them know upfront. If you don't, they will be busy wondering what it is they are meant to be doing, instead of listening to you.

4. What is the audience going to get as a result of listening?

This is a question you ignore at your peril. People always want to know what's in it for them. Quite right too. If they are going to give you their time and attention it makes sense that they want to know what they are going to get in return. So tell them.

Once again, the important thing here is to show that you have thought about it. Different people might, in reality, get quite different things from what you say, but what matters is showing that you have their interests in mind. This is different from trying to control how they respond. It is the demonstration of attention that helps create the connection.

Again, the possibilities are infinite. Bear in mind it isn't necessarily information you are giving them, it could be a new perspective, or entertainment, or the chance to disconnect from other worries.

5. Is the audience being seen or acknowledged?

Even though the presenter is in the spotlight, the audience still needs to be seen. Almost everyone forgets this and it has serious consequences. If an audience hasn't been seen they will often behave badly, in order to be seen. So communication breaks down. In improv shows there is always someone who at any request for a suggestion will shout 'Proctologist'. They don't really want to see a scene about a rectal examination, they want to be seen. Which is part of the reason that improvisers allow people to shout out suggestions.

In a business setting an audience will often raise awkward questions or objections in order to be seen. We will explore how you might deal with these in a moment, but it is important to realise that if you see the audience well in the first place, you will prevent many of these obstacles from occurring at all. This is particularly important if you want approval for a proposal of some kind. Make sure you acknowledge the audience early on, or they will make themselves seen big time by saying 'no' to whatever you are proposing.

With a presentation, this can be as simple as acknowledging that the room is half-empty, or packed to the gills, or that it is late. It doesn't necessarily have to be something the whole audience share. You can see a whole audience by picking out a detail and seeing one person, e.g. 'John told me as we were coming in that this has been a difficult week.' The rest of the audience will empathise.

This is exactly what is going on when a rock star at a stadium concert says, 'Good evening, Glastonbury!' If we are in the crowd we feel great because we feel seen. This isn't logical, even the most drug-fried rock star really *ought* to know where he is, but even so, the crowd loves it. A connection is created.

You can even use the reluctance of an audience to participate as a way of seeing them. When an attempt to connect is met by a stony silence, Adam Morgan will often say, 'I will take silence as a sign of enthusiastic assent,' using the audience's behaviour as an offer and seeing them in the process.

The Audience Requirements Grid (page 51) serves as a check list. Once you have something prepared, write down what you are planning to do to meet each of these needs in the first few minutes (which is where you win over - or lose

- the audience). It needn't be much; audience needs can be met very quickly, sometimes simultaneously.

It is very easy to do this but the chances are you will have forgotten something, which is why you do it in advance. This is where the grid comes in. It acts as a discipline. It reminds you that you need to think about it.

Without it I would normally forget to go through this thought process, even though I know how important it is. I still often forget until the last minute and find myself in the taxi on the way to a meeting hurriedly applying the grid. But even at this late stage it always helps. I invariably find something I had missed and make changes as a result. Improv isn't always about being spontaneous. The emphasis it puts on the audience's needs, above your own, provides us with tools like this that can help you prepare.

It is curious that we so easily forget to think about something as important as what the audience needs? Why is this?

One simple, if somewhat surprising, explanation is that we find other human beings scary. We worry enormously about what other people think of us. It is often said that what people most fear, after death, is public speaking. Facing an audience seems to elicit the same nervous response that our ancestors had when facing a sabre-toothed tiger.

So we look the other way. We invest the details (like bullet points or typefaces) with importance to avoid confronting the more difficult issues, sticking our head deep in the sand. Instead of focusing on what is important, we focus on what we can control, namely - the slides.

By contrast, improvisers understand that an audience, while scary, is also very supportive. They know that people do not like to watch failure, so at some level they want you to succeed.

This seems contradictory but I don't think it is. The stage itself is a useful metaphor. It is flat and supportive; but it has a sharp edge, not a gentle one. Step over this and you plummet into the orchestra pit. An audience is similar. If you take them into account, they will be supportive and forgiving. But fail to attend to their needs and they are ruthless. Their attention and engagement cuts off suddenly, just like the edge of the stage. Using the Audience Requirements Grid is a way to keep you away from that edge.

I don't mean to say that the role of content in a presentation is irrelevant. Good slides can lift things and great material can, occasionally, carry the day. For example, there is a magnificent TED talk (see www.ted.com) by statistician Hans Rosling whose animated visualisation of data is stunning. But these animations were the result of decades of work. And, realising that there is more to presentations than good data, at the end, Rosling strips off to reveal a spandex vest and goes on to swallow a sword (or to be more accurate, a 19th-century Swedish infantry bayonet). Really. Check it out.

Going Off Piste

Something we are often asked to help people with is how to deal with objections or questions. People find this scary because questions and objections lie beyond their control. But if you really want to communicate, offers from the audience, of any kind, are a godsend. An aggressive question can be a thumping big offer, if you are willing to treat it as such. Moreover, responding well to such curve balls is one of the quickest and most effective ways to connect with an audience.

The first thing is to let go of knowing everything. Much of the anxiety people feel comes from the sensation that they have to respond to everything and, in the case of questions, be able to answer them. Give up the idea that you have to be able to respond perfectly and instantly to everything, it only inhibits you. Allow yourself to not know. Moreover, some questions can't be answered, some objections don't deserve your attention, some things aren't appropriate to deal with in public and some things, however interesting, don't suit your purpose in the moment.

So the first important thing in being able to respond well is to know what matters to you at that moment, to have a clear grasp of your purpose and how unfolding events serve or impede your progress towards it. Improvisers do this all the time. A superficial understanding suggests that improvisers say 'yes' to everything but that isn't true. They are constantly choosing which offers to accept and which to block based on a feel for what the story needs next. They will quite deliberately block offers that feel like blind alleys or distract from the main thrust of the story. They do so quickly and instinctively and work on developing a feel for the offers that feed their purpose. You can do the same.

I have just come back from working with a Disaster Response team in Asia. During one session I was asked how the cultural complexities around saying 'yes' or 'no' played out in different Asian cultures. I tried to answer it. Which was a mistake. I don't know anything about Asian cultures so my response was vague, unhelpful and made me look foolish. I had been seduced by my position. Being at the front of the room made me feel that I ought to answer, so I did. I would have done much better to follow Mark Twain's example: 'I was asked a difficult question and I was delighted to be able to answer at once: "I don't know," I said.'

Twenty minutes later, I did exactly that. I was asked another tricky question, about how to react to the deception and deceit that can occur during disasters. Fresh from the earlier embarrassment, I answered with a block. I pointed out that other people in the room were much better placed to address that question than me and that it didn't serve our purpose to address such a huge and complex question with 40 people in the middle of a workshop. Heads nodded all around the room, including the head of the person who had posed the question.

So blocking has a place. It is occasionally a legitimate response. You can use it to help you let go of the idea you have to answer everything immediately, and that will help you deal with the anxiety that difficult questions can provoke.

Most of the time, however, you will want to create flow, so you won't want to block. No prizes for guessing this means noticing more, letting go and using everything. Listening is hardly a radical suggestion, but the trouble is that when faced by a question or objection we often don't do it. The anxiety of being put on the spot can make the mind race, or go blank. It is all too easy to veer off into your own thoughts, or leap ahead to a prepared response, or answer a different question. Instead, make a conscious effort to listen to the actual question you are being asked, by this person, in this moment.

Your body is your friend (and ally) here. Use it. Breathe, lean forward or tilt your head towards the questioner and make eye contact. Find whichever physical cues work for you (which is part of the ongoing practice of noticing more about how you hold and use your body). Listen to the tone as well as the content. Notice everything you can about how it is being asked. Listen for the emphasis, or energy, or emotion - these are part of the question too.

Listening intently in this way gives you pause, and shows the person asking (and their question) respect. Slowing down brings you into the present and reminds you to let go of shadow stories or expectations. This gives you a little bit of time to be with the question before you launch into a response. It isn't enough time to think, plan, or analyse consciously, but it is enough to allow your unconscious, which works much faster, to get going. If you really listen, you will find you have more resources to draw on than you might expect.

Listening also has a significant effect on the questioner. Sometimes, in fact, listening is *all* that is needed. Being heard and acknowledged is sometimes more important than receiving an answer. Many 'difficult' questions are, as we saw above, really about a desire to be seen.

Having listened, you are in a position to treat the question as an offer. Don't leap to conclusions about why the question is being asked, or judge the person asking it. Let go of whatever shadow story leaps up at this moment. The motivations and intentions of the questioner may be good, bad or indifferent, but you cannot be sure of what they are so trying to double guess won't help you respond. Let go of all that judgement and, instead, simply regard the question as an offer. Which means finding a way to use it.

As ever, regard something as an offer and it becomes one. There are lots of ways to use a question or objection. Try answering a question with another question (which, coincidentally, is another improv game).
For example, you might say:

— What makes you ask that?
— What would your answer be?
— Does anyone else have the same question?

— I have no idea. Does anyone else?
— Who is best qualified to answer that?

Unlike presentations, where most people keep their thoughts to themselves, in workshops people sometimes get very aggressive and say things like, 'This is stupid, it's a complete waste of time.' Years ago, this kind of response would bother me, but now, perversely perhaps, I rather like it. There is tons of energy and emotion in such a comment and the person making it is normally being both brave and honest. Which is a great offer.

Both for the person objecting and for the rest of the group it is very powerful if you can accept their response, rather than trying to argue with them. I might ask why they think what we are doing is stupid, why it is a waste of time, or what it would mean to not waste time. Try not to make them wrong. Who knows, they might in fact be right and through the inquiry we might be able to change or adjust what we do to good effect.

Often the fear of objections or questions comes from an excessive focus on getting through our stuff. The trouble is, this is pointless unless your stuff is getting through to those present. Once again, if you are only talking to yourself, you aren't communicating, however tranquil it may feel or however polished it may come across. Questions and objections to what you are saying allow you to get real-time feedback and input and you can adjust accordingly; then you are really communicating.

It seems to me there is a great irony at the heart of the difficulties we have around communication. We want to create a connection with an audience, and yet we devise all sorts of shields and barriers, like Powerpoint, to protect or distance ourselves from them. At heart, communication is

COMMUNICATION

a very simple business that we tend to over-complicate.

Improvisers have given us a number of specific tools that can help us communicate better, particularly in proto-theatrical settings, like presentations.

However, more importantly, they have given us a way of looking that makes the basic building blocks of communication both visible and comprehensible. The modest set of ideas and behaviours expressed in the basic practices is of untold value. Apply it to your communication and you could be using it all day long for the rest of your life.

GAME

'YES, AND ...'

'Yes, and ...' is, in many ways, the archetypal improv game. It captures many of the important features of the way improvisers work.

At a glance	Group tell a story using 'Yes, and ...' to connect each beat.
Purpose	Show the difference between accepting and blocking - make visible how often we block without realising ('yes, but' versus 'yes, and'). Demonstrate the dramatic power of blocks.
Mechanics	Group of 6-15 people in a circle. Rest of group observe.
Set-up	Seat people, explain that each person has to say 'Yes, and ...' to what came before and add something to it.
Debrief	What did we see in terms of accepting and blocking? What happened to the story as a result? How does this show up at work?

HOW THE GAME WORKS

There are lots of different ways you can play 'Yes, and ...' I normally use a group of somewhere between 6 and 15 people, seated in a circle. Everyone else observes. You explain that we are going to tell a story together. Someone will start with a very simple beginning like 'It was raining hard.' The next person must do two things - acknowledge what has come before and add something to it. They always begin by saying 'Yes, and ...'

It works like this:

   'It was raining hard.'

   'Yes, and … John was getting soaked.'

It then passes to the third person, who might add:

   *'Yes, and … since he was wet through John began to get
   cold, so he decided to walk home instead of wait for the bus.'*

And so on. Keep the story going as long as there is energy for it
or until it reaches a natural conclusion. Coach people to avoid 'I'
statements, which are confusing in a group game.

THINGS TO WATCH OUT FOR

Along the way, watch out for people saying 'Yes, but …' instead
of 'Yes, and …' They do this all the time (which speaks volumes
about how we normally behave). Insist on them saying the
words 'Yes, and …' rather than skipping them. Especially if they
are struggling - voicing those words can help to get them going.

It is important that each person demonstrates they have
listened by using what came immediately before.

Consider this contribution for example:

   'It was raining hard.'

   'Yes, and … John was getting soaked.'

   'Yes, and … a car crashed.'

The car crashing has a very weak connection to the beat before
(rain = dangerous roads?) so you would pause the story and

invite that person to have another go, reminding them to use the idea that John was getting soaked. Do this in a supportive, not a critical way.

If someone very obviously blocks, by contradicting what came before (which people *will* do), be gentle on them, but remind them of what came before and invite them to build on that, not change it. When my business partner Gary runs this he warns people that he is going to 'side coach' insistently and that they will be fed up with him by the end of the exercise. By forewarning them he takes the sting out of it.

It also helps if, at the outset, you explain that the storytellers (who are normally volunteers) are there to help the rest of us. They are not there so that we can evaluate or test them, but to create something (a story) that we can all examine, which is a generous act. The real work here, you say, is going to be done by the audience. That shifts the responsibility and makes sure the people watching stay engaged.

DEBRIEF

Ask where the story was satisfying, where it wasn't and why. See if you can get them to identify what it was people were doing that made the story work, or falter. Normally I ask the audience first, then the players themselves. It is interesting to compare and contrast the outside and the inside view.

You can ask about anything and everything that people did and the effect it had on the story (which is a metaphor for whatever relationship, product or project that people are engaged in for real).

For example:
— Where did the story flow? Why?
— Where did the story falter? Why?

— Which bits did we like most? Why?
— What was the effect of listening (or not) on the story and on how we felt about that person?
— How did we know if someone was or wasn't listening?
— Could we see people planning ahead? What effect did that have?
— What happened when someone blocked?
— What was the story missing?
— What was the effect of how people said things - body language, the speed or slowness with which they responded?
— For the players, what was hard about that? What was easy? Why?

If you are facilitating, you will have your own answers to any of these questions, which are worth sharing. One thing to look out for that a group rarely notices is the value of 'connective tissue'. Often the most pleasing bits of the story are when someone simply joins together things which were there already, often through extended listening. This is far more important than being 'original'.

WHEN TO USE 'YES, AND ...'

'Yes, and ...' is a game that forces people to accept. This is useful in two ways. First, it makes visible the effects of blocking and accepting on the story. Secondly, it shows how hard people find it to accept and how they often block without realising. It is amazing how many people automatically say 'yes, but' instead of 'yes, and'.

Like Presents, this game is essentially about accepting, blocking and flow, but it has a very different mood. With 'Yes, and ...' there is pressure and the performance anxiety that comes with it, which raises the stakes. 'Yes, and ...' makes the implications of accepting and blocking publicly visible. It doesn't generate the same warmth and energy as Presents, so use it when you want to get clarity around these practices and really spell them out.

VARIATIONS

There is a variation of 'Yes, and …' which involves a very clear and potent demonstration of blocking. You join the circle yourself (or get a stooge).

Once the story has been running for a while, and it gets to you, you block deliberately, like this:

> 'Yes, and … when John finally got home he got himself a beer immediately.'
>
> 'No he didn't.'

At this point the person who gave you the offer will almost certainly respond in one of three ways:

1. They are crushed and don't know what to do.
2. They try to assert themselves by saying, 'Yes he did.'
3. They try and use your block as an offer by saying something like, 'That's right, he remembered he had given up booze so made himself a cup of tea.'

Most people fall into the second category. If someone is naturally good at creating flow they might fall into the third category. At which point, if you really want to make a point, you can block them again. This is a pretty strong move, so when you choose where to join the circle, make sure the person you are planning to block isn't fragile (I once really upset somebody because I didn't think about this). Once the block has landed, stop and have a debrief. In that debrief, if someone has responded well by using your block as an offer make it visible and acknowledge them for it. You can use it to highlight how powerful a piece of behaviour it is in an organisation.

The point of this is to show the power of a block and where the weight of it falls (on the person receiving, in case you had any doubt). Ask people what happened when you blocked and they get it immediately - they see that it cuts the flow, creates confusion and conflict, affects the other person negatively and so on. You can then ask them to think of a block from their everyday life. Once they have one, get them to raise their hands if their example is one where they are doing the blocking themselves. Hardly anyone will raise their hands. This emphasises the point that we don't notice or give importance to the blocks we dish out, but to the ones we receive.

You can also play 'Yes, and ...' in small groups, but pairs isn't to be recommended because it is too easy to keep the story on your agenda. Three is the minimum. I tend not to do this though because I deliberately prefer to use 'Yes, and ...' in the very public way I have described here.

This is another game we learned from Keith Johnstone.

4
Creativity

Creativity sets humans apart. Everything we make or do depends on our creative history. From stone axes to supercolliders, the ability to create things for ourselves is one of our defining characteristics.

From axes we moved on to fire, arrows, pots, agriculture, cooking, recipes, cuisine, nouvelle cuisine and so on, all the way up to the celebrity chef. Along the way we created art, science, philosophy and rubbish bags with little drawstrings that make them easier to close (one of my personal favourites). By being creative we have shaped and fashioned the world around us to an enormous extent.

If creativity is our past, it is also our future. According to Sir Ken Robinson, Emeritus Professor of Education at Warwick University, 'creativity is the new literacy'. It is *that* important. In a global economy, driven by rapid technological change, creativity at every level is fundamental. Organisations of all kinds, including businesses, governments and NGOs, constantly need to create new products and services, or find new ways to deliver old ones. Or, to reinvent themselves completely.

The same is true for individuals, who need to become

more creative not just to keep themselves employable but in order to shape their lives, which will not proceed along the predictable, professional paths that they used to. As Robinson points out, most of the children in school today will do jobs that haven't been invented yet. This is new.

Ironically enough, we are also going to have to become very creative in order to clean up the mess that our industrial-scale creativity has produced thus far. We have to find ways to make things that don't create toxic waste, squander energy or destroy the ecosystems on which we depend to grow food, cycle water or produce oxygen. Just doing less of what we currently do won't be enough. We need to be radically creative.

Furthermore, all the most interesting and important human dilemmas, like how to reconcile liberty and security, are problems that we can never 'solve'. Instead of single answers, we have to come up with a stream of creative responses, as we adapt anew to changing circumstances. The demand for creativity will never diminish.

More subtly, creativity is also important to the present, to the quality of life that we experience in every moment. This is significant because, as I mentioned earlier, the present is where we live. Psychologist Mihaly Csikszentmihalyi, who has dedicated his career to the study of happiness and creativity, argues that 'to have a good life it is not enough to remove what is wrong with it'. Happiness, it seems, is about more than solving problems. In order to be happy, we need to find ways to express and develop our creativity. Creativity, it turns out, matters an awful lot.

––––––––

Given this importance, it is worrisome that the popular image of creativity is about as misleading as it is widespread.

Ask most people to conjure up an idea of someone creative and they will come up with a version of the 'eccentric inventor' or 'artist in his garret'. In fact, the *New Oxford American Dictionary* even defines a garret as 'a small, dismal attic or top floor room traditionally inhabited by an artist'.

We think of a lone individual, with rare talent, odd dress sense, outrageous personality and, perhaps, dubious morals, engaged in a tortuous process of creation, with inspiration occurring in blinding flashes. This is the 'creative' from Hollywood central casting and I have known plenty of copywriters eager to live up to it.

There are two striking features of this image. First, it is not a very accurate depiction of how creativity occurs, either in the arts or in science (or, for that matter, in business). It certainly bears no resemblance to what happens on the improv stage. Secondly, it depicts creative people as 'other'. They are disconnected and separate.

If you hold this image, it is unlikely you will think of yourself as creative. Which is inhibiting. It stops you being, or becoming, as creative as you might. To paraphrase Henry Ford - if you believe you aren't creative, you'll be right. We need to debunk this image.

Let's start with the pain. It may indeed be difficult to make a living as an *artist*, but that doesn't mean the *creative* process itself is a necessarily painful one. Struggle may be involved, but in many ways play is more important to creativity than pain, as we shall see. Improvisers have an enormous amount of fun while they create. It's a large part of why they do it.

The idea that you are born creative (or not) is another unhelpful one. I often hear professional creative people promote it. This is hardly surprising, since it makes them 'special'. However, for those who aren't professional creatives, it sets up a self-fulfilling prophesy. If creativity is an innate talent, you would be a fool to try and develop it, so, lo and behold, you don't.

It is more helpful to think like the ancient Greeks. They suggested that people were 'visited' by the muse. For centuries, inspiration was a touch of the divine. It came and went. It was neither a talent, nor a possession - it wasn't yours alone.

In fact, this is much more accurate than creativity being regarded as a special talent. Creative people rarely work in isolation. There is always a milieu - a movement or a community of some kind, where ideas are sparked off, exchanged, cross-fertilised and tested. This may be informal, like the coffee houses of 17th-century London, or formal, like the modern scientific peer review process, but one way or another there is interaction between people and their ideas.

This is very obvious with improvisers, whose creative process is visibly collective, but even when someone appears to be isolated, they still interact with other people's ideas, through reading or correspondence. It is neat and tidy to attribute acts of creation to individuals (and it normally suits the individuals concerned) but there is almost always a collaborative element. The individual is always in a context - and ideas emerge from the relationship between the people who operate in that context.

If creativity is to become the new literacy, we have some work to do. Using improvisation as a source of inspiration is one good way to challenge many of the assumptions we make about creativity. It also provides some specific pointers about practical things we can do to develop our creative abilities.

In this chapter I am going to explore four of these ideas:

1 The importance of play
2 Creative doing, not creative thinking
3 Putting flow first
4 Embracing constraint

Let's have a look at each in turn.

The Importance of Play

The Comedy Store Players have been performing a high-quality, improvised show to satisfied paying customers twice a week for over 20 years. This adds up to thousands of hours of relentless creativity. There are many groups like this, all around the world. Improvisers reliably and consistently deliver a profitable, highly creative product, over long periods of time. Which is something of a holy grail in business.

If this ability were mercurial and mysterious there would be nothing to do but sit back and applaud. Yet improvisers draw on a body of knowledge that enables them to do this. It is not luck or accident. The question is, what do they know that we can borrow or emulate? What do they do that stops them behaving like a committee?

Improvisers mostly perform comedy. Which means that they tend not to take themselves too seriously. They are happy to play around. The rest of us should take note. We don't enjoy the same advantage. We tend to take our work (and ourselves) more seriously. 'I am a senior executive in an important business, I can't be larking around like a clown,' is the kind of belief that many of us hold dear. Play is neither part of our job description, nor our self-image.

If you want to become more creative, you need to change that. Or at least be willing to let it go from time to time. John Cleese has suggested that creativity is not so much a special talent, as a willingness to play.

Play is more than just fun (though we will get to that). Play is important, because it opens the door to new possibilities. New ideas are, by definition, strange at first. Through play we explore what they might have to offer. We flirt with the unknown.

Allow yourself to be playful. Entertain ideas that you would normally dismiss, even if it is only for a few moments. Using 'everything' includes those things that might seem silly, so keep new or unusual possibilities 'in play' and see where they take you.

Don't cling on too tight to knowing what you want or you will never allow yourself to discover anything else. If Alexander Fleming had, he wouldn't have discovered penicillin. How do you know whether something will become relevant? Allow a playful attitude to loosen you up, to help you 'let go'.

Play around with things at the edge of what is normal or known. Read a magazine you would never normally pick up. *Rabbit Owners Monthly* will show you a whole world you didn't know existed (and thus, if nothing else, the limits to your own). Speak to someone you don't know. Eat different food. Allow yourself to wander off rather than always 'pushing on'. Look up. Look sideways. Fertile territory often lies in the margins or overlaps. If you are too direct, or in too much of a hurry, you will never come across them.

Playfulness also helps you to stop self-censoring your own ideas. If you are only 'playing' it doesn't matter so much how you come across. It is easier to stop worrying about whether you sound stupid. Musicians jam and lark around until something definable emerges. Apparently the famous riff in the Queen song 'Another One Bites the Dust' was 'discovered' this way.

The fact that play is fun ought to be an additional plus - after all, it seems to have a lot going for it. It makes life enjoyable. It invokes and engages the whole person: left brain, right brain, body and all. It connects us to other people, with whom we collaborate as well as compete, so that we build relationships as well as ideas. Our efforts add up. Energy and laughter are released. Improvisers understand these principles much better than many of us.

For example, Gary, my business partner in On Your Feet, constantly asks himself, 'Am I enjoying this?' He does this moment by moment, day by day, year by year. He regards fun as a perfectly valid measure and believes that if he is having fun, then he will be more effective. Research in the field of positive psychology would suggest he is right.

If he isn't having fun, he will change what he is doing. This doesn't mean giving up, or going off in a huff, it means asking himself how he could act differently to make things more fun. This requires presence of mind and discipline. It also requires being willing to be changed (i.e. being prepared to be wrong).

The result is that Gary has a better time at work than almost anyone I know. It also gives him strategic direction. He consistently navigates by assessing how satisfying and rewarding the work he is doing is. Which is a very healthy principle.

By contrast, for most of us, fun is a barrier. It makes us see play as trivial, or childish. We believe that we shouldn't be happy, or have fun at work. When I work with senior executives, it is striking how many of them are deeply uncomfortable and highly suspicious of play. As a result they enjoy neither the play itself, nor any of its benefits.

This rather perverse attitude owes something to puritans and engineers (both strong influences on the culture of modern business). To puritans, work is virtuous whereas play is indulgent and sinful. The two are separate and opposed, so play has no place at work. Engineers add another negative interpretation. To an engineer, 'play' is looseness in a mechanism, so you don't want too much, or things become sloppy. Precision is good, play is bad. No wonder we find it hard to engage in play.

If you want to become more creative, a willingness to play is something that you need to cultivate, both individually and collectively. Not as a distraction or a reward, but as part of the work itself. Given the public image of play, that takes commitment and a certain amount of courage. It's a tough job, but somebody has to do it. It might as well be you.

Creative Doing, Not Creative Thinking

When people in business talk to me about creativity, they normally talk about creative thinking. Improvisers, by contrast, don't have much time for creative thinking. Their focus is on creative *doing*. As actors, what matters to them is action. An audience won't pay to watch someone think, however creative their thoughts might be.

Ultimately, action is what counts in business too. You have to reformulate the ingredients, or make new packaging, or get people to behave differently when they answer the phone. To be creative we have to *do* something, not just think, or talk, about doing it. Creativity is embodied. It is physical not abstract. You can't be creative just by thinking.

There are a couple of reasons why business people get hooked on creative thinking rather than creative doing. First, there is a belief that thought is primary, and that action must follow it. The assumption is that if you want to act creatively you must *first* think creatively (an impression amplified by Apple's famous 'Think Different' campaign). The second is that it is an awful lot easier to think about doing something than to actually do it. If you can convince yourself that creative thinking is what actually matters (and ignore the creative doing bit) you make things seem a whole lot easier.

As a result, it is easy to over-think things. A lot of energy and attention is devoted to thinking differently but little of it translates into action. There is plenty that is 'interesting' but nothing much changes. No one learns very fast.

The alternative, which is what improvisers practise, is to focus on creative *doing*. It is just as valid, and far more effective, to act yourself into a new way of thinking, rather than trying to think yourself into a new way of acting (which is what we normally do). This is absurdly simple but quite a challenge. The idea that thinking comes first is so automatic that we struggle to see how it could be any other way.

Acting first doesn't mean being thoughtless or foolhardy. It means doing things before you know precisely how they work. It means physically committing to an action and allowing ideas to emerge. Nietzsche, himself a great thinker, famously suggested that all great ideas are conceived by walking. Since body and mind are integrated, not separate, ideas can just as well flow from the body to the mind as the other way round. Both paths are valid.

Improvisers will step into a scene *before* they have an idea. They may make a gesture or movement, without defining either to the audience, or to themselves, what it is that they are doing. Only when another actor says, 'Looks like you're having trouble opening that tin,' do we discover what it is (or to be more accurate, what it has *become*). By committing to action we allow someone else to add their own interpretation, which may be one we would never have thought of. Thus we get creative.

You want new ideas for next year's strategy? Don't sit at your desk. Walk the factory floor or visit the shop. Phone your own customer service line and see how you get treated. Get your hands on the product (or your competitors') and play around with it, so that you *really* get to know it.

Try reframing your consumer research as action not talk. Instead of testing ideas with consumers, find the people who use the product a lot and watch what they do with it, for real. Find out what matters to them and what could be made better through the doing. Don't ask them what they think, watch what they do. Or better still, join in and play around with them yourselves.

A group of car engineers, who were all men, but who were designing a car for women, did exactly that. The female consumers suggested that one of the engineers acted out a woman getting into her car (for fun they insisted it was the one who had a beard). When the bearded 'woman' walked up to the (imaginary) car and put his (imaginary) handbag down on the ground while he unlocked the car door, the women all screamed, 'You don't *ever* do that!' Putting their handbag down was unthinkable. This prompted a rich and creative conversation about issues of security, ways of unlocking the car and so on. Making the action visible created possibilities that would not have occurred if they had just been talking about it. The women would never have mentioned this because it was so obvious to them. Acting first also means not trying to anticipate. Anticipation slows things down. It is much better to try stuff out. Make a model or a prototype as soon as you can and see how it works. If what you make isn't tangible, design an experiment or game, instead of a model. One way or another, play your idea out. Learn from the experience. Incorporate that learning, then make a new prototype. That's what design studio IDEO, one of the world's most creative companies, does. They make prototypes of whatever they are designing as soon as they can. Their motto is 'fail early, fail often'. If you want to be creative it is much better to focus on 'safe to fail', which means small-scale experiments with rapid feedback. This is very different from a focus on 'fail-safe', where caution and conservatism predominate.

Years back I worked as a consultant for a drinks company on new product development. The desire to be sure about everything made it painfully slow. There were umpteen rounds of concept development and consumer testing. Meanwhile, in a backwater of the same company, a few ingenious souls would mock something up, take it down to a bar and see what flew. Not only were they the ones who came up with the ground-breaking innovations, but they had a blast doing it. I wish I could say the same.

These renegade drinks developers knew what improvisers know - that the importance of creative thinking is exaggerated. If you want to get creative, don't just sit there and think about it, *do* something.

The easiest thing to do is move. It is also, quite possibly, the most productive. This is the direction I most frequently give people in workshops. It is often the *only* direction I need to give people.

When you move, a lot happens. You see things from a different angle. The light falls differently, different sounds reach you, you touch a different surface or feel a different movement of air, with a different scent or temperature. You receive a wealth of new information. When you move, you shift your point of view.

You change your internal environment too. Blood pumps and muscles contract. Your senses, which are only really interested in change, become more alert. Millions of nerve cells fire. Different sensations lead to different feelings. Changing your posture or position changes what you receive, and how you perceive it. This all happens very fast. It is automatic and powerful.

Sit in a different chair. Stand up. Lie down. Walk around the block. If you want a more creative meeting, move people around. Don't let them get comfortably stuck in a particular chair, or their ideas will get comfortably stuck as well.

If it feels too strange to do this explicitly, be sneaky. Have frequent breaks, move furniture, disturb the physical layout so that people can't stay put, sit somewhere else yourself (to create a domino effect) or break them into groups or pairs for conversations. Variation and physical movement helps people stay alert as well as increasing the chances of them having a new idea.

A beautiful example of the power of movement (and being playful) is a TED talk by John Bohannon called 'Dance your PhD'. In a moment of playfulness a scientist invited some dancers to help him communicate his ideas physically. What starts off as an irreverent means of illustrating ideas turns, quite unexpectedly, into something far more powerful. In order to bring the ideas to life, the dancers, with their focus on the physical body, have a very different point of view to the scientists and started to ask questions that none of researchers would ever have thought of. This input changed the direction of the scientific work itself and gave the scientists new insights and ideas. Which just goes to show, when it comes to creativity, it is all very well having a powerful brain, but there's nothing quite like a good body.

Putting Flow First

People often say, 'There is no such thing as a bad idea.'
I beg to differ. If there were no such thing as a bad idea,
semi-automatic weapons would not be freely available
over the counter in the world's richest country. If every
idea was a good idea, we wouldn't need to become any
more creative. But that isn't the case. There are plenty of
ideas which are bad ideas. I know, because I have them all
the time myself. We all do.

What *is* important is not to judge ideas as soon as they
appear. If we judge ideas immediately, we don't just kill
them, we kill all the other ideas and possibilities that they
might give rise to. Which is why animation studio Pixar's
philosophy is 'from suck to unsuck'. This acknowledges
that the first ideas are likely to 'suck'. I think this is helpful.
I find the claim that 'there is no such thing as a bad idea'
wrong-headed and cheesy. Instead, I prefer to say, 'There
is no such thing as a good idea ... *yet*.' This adds something
else. It suggests that no idea is born complete, whole and
perfect. The '... yet' is important. It puts the emphasis
on what we *do* with ideas, which takes the pressure off
the idea itself. Whether your first idea is good, bad or
indifferent, it will still need to develop, evolve, maybe even
transform. Any idea, like any living thing, needs to grow.

Improvisers achieve this by paying attention to flow.
Their first instinct is to get going. They know that the
audience wants to see something happen, so they take
whatever they have and use it to begin their story. If they
have an apple they take a bite. Or stuff it in the mouth of
the pig they are roasting. Or use it to discover gravity, or
tempt Eve.

What they do is less important than the fluency
with which they do it. They know and understand the

importance of momentum to the creative process. They appreciate that ideas can evolve very quickly once you create flow. Conversely, they are aware that pursuing perfection can lead to paralysis. They know that agonising over whether something is right will hurt you and the process (as the word 'agonising' itself suggests).

At the heart of this is the practice of accepting. To accept an offer is to take something, thereby acknowledging it, and then to do something with it. This generates flow. You extend your hand, I shake it. You tell me you are pregnant, I congratulate you (or commiserate, depending on the circumstances). Accepting an offer connects two ideas, builds on them and leads to more possibilities. It gives impetus to the process. It acknowledges and includes other people by using their ideas, rather than ignoring or marginalising them. This encourages them to make more contributions. The archetypal improv game of 'Yes, and …' captures the essence of this. If the rest of us could substitute our propensity to say 'yes, but' for 'yes, and' we would become a lot more creative.

If we accept ideas rather than block them they have the chance to go somewhere. We set in motion an evolutionary process and our first ideas become the parents (then grandparents and great-grandparents) of a great number of other ideas. This is why it is important not to judge them immediately. When we knock an idea on the head, we kill all its offspring too. We need the fluency that accepting ideas brings, because the best way to make sure you have good ideas is to have lots of (good and bad) ideas. Accepting is neither passive nor weak. There are plenty of different ways you can accept any particular offer, as the example with the apple above demonstrates.

Thinking of ideas as parents of other ideas also reminds

us that, just as we do with our own children, we have to let them go, stop trying to control them and see what wants to emerge (which is easier if you regard them as a gift from the muse in the first place).

This is particularly true once they start to get fleshed out. The creative process doesn't stop just because we have started to make something (or 'execute' in the rather morbid business jargon). We have to be prepared to keep on letting go because during the process of realisation an idea may be transformed further, often to good effect.

Michelangelo made many preparatory sketches for his paintings. Yet his idea of preparation was very flexible. He wrote about the importance of not being wedded to an initial idea or plan and continued to extemporise and develop his ideas while he worked on a painting, so that the final work might be very far from the early studies. Art historians find it hard to say at what stage his work stops being preparatory.

Michelangelo was also famous for failing to 'finish' many of his works, which I think is to be recommended. During a creative process leaving thoughts or ideas unfinished does two things. It invites other people to finish them. In doing so, there is a good chance that they will add something you hadn't thought of, and enrich the idea in the process. This in turn takes the pressure off you, because you don't have to shoulder all the responsibility, which in turn allows you to become more fluent, more open and less controlling.

Accepting is also vital to the creative climate. When ideas are habitually or routinely blocked, it crushes the people that contributed them, as well as the ideas themselves. Accepting creates flow and that takes you somewhere. If you don't like where you are, but you stay in flow, you will get somewhere else soon enough. By contrast, blocking stops you where you are. It reduces possibility and increases stress. It produces conflict and confusion. It cuts people and ideas off from one another.

To be fair, blocking can be an important behaviour, just not when you are trying to generate new ideas. It comes into its own when you are winnowing them down or trying to reach a conclusion. But it isn't the place to start.

The simple lesson from all of this is that if we want to become more creative, we need to focus on getting going, before we worry about getting it right.

Embracing Constraint

Improvisers are fond of making things hard for themselves. Not only do they do without a script, but they embrace additional constraints, which seem to make their task more difficult. For example, 'last letter, first letter'. This is a scene where the first word of every speech has to start with the same letter of the alphabet as the last letter of the last word of the previous speech.

Like this:

Matt: Do you take sugar?

Daryl: Regrettably, I do, even though it's bad for me.

Matt: Everything's bad for you.

Daryl: Usually.

Matt: You look worried.

Daryl: Duh. I mean, you would look worried if Charlene was after you. She discovered I cheated on her.

Matt: Rrrrrrreally, she found out?

Daryl: Too late now, she's on the warpath.

... And so on.

Matt and Daryl have to invent characters, relationships and events to make a coherent story and, in addition, follow the rule of 'last letter, first letter'. This looks so difficult that it wins them the goodwill of the audience before they even begin. Which is handy, but it isn't why they do it.

What the audience doesn't realise is that the constraint is there to give them some structure to work with. This has the double benefit of making it look more difficult while actually making it easier.

Think about what this constraint obliges them to do. They have to wait for the other person to finish in order to know which letter they have to use. That stops them hurrying, or planning, and forces them to be present.

They listen better, which gives them more information to work with. They are literally obliged to notice more. They have a concrete start point, or 'handhold', and this cuts down the number of options they have to deal with, which gives them direction. If they wish, they can start simply by committing to the sound and allow an idea to come from that (something I indicated here with the 'Rrrrrrreally' above).

Creativity is stimulated by embracing constraint; not by a complete absence of constraints. In the arts, it is often the materials used that present limitations and constraints - whether it's clay or canvas or the sound of a sax. Improv games invariably involve limitation of some kind. You can only say one word or when one actor stands the other has to sit (and vice versa). These impositions stimulate creativity because they provide something to rub up against. The constraint gives the mind traction and that creates impetus. It is much harder for improvisers to create a scene or story with no suggestion from the audience and nothing at all to limit them.

Creativity is about making choices and, when you can go anywhere, it is much harder to choose. For example, in workshops, when people get stuck it is not because they can't think of anything to say or do. It is because there are too many things they could say or do and they clam up trying to decide which one to choose. Too many options make us anxious. When the Berlin Wall came down, East German housewives broke down in tears in West German supermarkets, not out of envy at the opulence of the West, but out of confusion - they had no way of making sense of the vast array of choices on offer and this provoked anxiety.

This is even harder when we obsess about making the 'right' choice - by which we normally mean the one that will make us look good (or clever, or funny). Embracing constraints gets beyond these unhelpful pre-judgements about whether your idea is a good or a bad one.

Understand this and it becomes easier to be creative. Don't flee from constraint, learn to use constraints constructively and seek them out. Let's try it now. Think of something you need new ideas about. Got something? I am going to do the same. My issue is how to engage more actively with my On Your Feet colleagues in America, without getting on a plane. Since we each have our own clients the relationship has become dormant and we don't learn from each other or work together as much, or as well, as we might.

Now, let's take an everyday object that is to hand. I am going to take the coffee cup that I have here on the table. We are going to use that as a constraint to get new ideas. Here's how. We forget, for the moment, about our issue, and focus on the coffee cup.

First, we list attributes and qualities of the coffee cup - plain, obvious things. I am also going to introduce another useful constraint here - time. You will have to take my word for it, but I get two minutes, no more, to list whatever comes to my mind about the coffee cup.

Here goes.

White, round, drips, rings, sediment, dregs, container, handle, everyday, hot, distraction, everyday, leftovers/dregs, smooth, drug, ceramic, hot, narrow, cheap, simple.

It doesn't matter that I repeated some words - what matters is letting them out quickly. Here comes the creative bit. You take these words and collide them with your issue. Remember, my issue is resuscitating the relationship with my US colleagues. I ask myself, 'How could that be white? What would it mean if that were white?' I have to let go of being literal, ignore the fact that it sounds like nonsense, embrace the constraint and force it onto my issue.

This only takes a few seconds. Starting with 'white' sets off a stream of consciousness that went like this:

White, white sheet of paper, blank sheet of paper, we should start again, relaunch the relationship, instead of taking it for granted or trying to have it evolve, create an event or an artefact to relaunch myself to them, like a menu of the things I could do for them, yes, in the form of a menu, as if they were ordering takeaway, an Indian restaurant-style menu.

A white coffee cup got me to realise that I need to disrupt the relationship and send a concrete signal of change and then to the specific idea of a mock Indian takeaway menu of services. In the context of On Your Feet, where humour and levity are part of our brand personality, it is quite an appropriate, practical idea.

It took much longer to type this up than it did to do (even though I type fast). Along the way, in a matter of seconds, I also got two other ideas - from 'drips', the idea of a drip 'campaign' - regular, small drops of information that put me on the radar of my American friends. From 'round', the idea of a Skype round-table session to share learning or client contacts.

So if you want to get new ideas, find a way to embrace constraint. Connect or collide constraints of different kinds into your issue. Use whatever you have to hand, from a coffee cup to a sales director or a two-hour deadline.

You need enough freedom to question assumptions, but wide-open vistas of possibility are less productive than combining things that normally don't go together. Ask, 'If the mafia ran our company, how would they act?' Instead of bridling under a constraint push it further, by asking, 'If we had to cut the time and budget for the project in half, what would we do?'

There are all sorts of constraints you can use, not just everyday objects. Make yourself an image bank - a deck of hundreds of images (from paintings to news pictures). You can buy these, but better to make one (you will be able to use it over and over again). If you do decide to make one, get a wide range of images and avoid using images from advertising, which are too slick or contrived. *National Geographic* magazine is a brilliant source of images.

Use people that don't know or share the conventional assumptions. Ask the sales director about R&D or the R&D people about a sales issue. Herb Kelleher, founder of the only consistently profitable airline in America, Southwest Airlines, was a lawyer.

Use constraints in time. If you have an hour to come up with ideas, don't design an exercise that lasts an hour. Do six different exercises for ten minutes each, or the same ten-minute exercise six times.

If you can do this, it not only fuels your creative process but it changes how you feel about constraints. Instead of being problems you start to see them as offers, which is perhaps the single most creative thing you can do.

Improvisation suggests that if you want to become a more creative individual you need to be less of an individual. That in a sense, all creativity is co-creativity. While this is a generalisation, it is nonetheless a useful counterpoint to the prevailing impression that creativity depends upon possession of a special talent that you have, or lack, from birth. It releases you from the burden of having sole responsibility for your own creative powers and shifts the emphasis on to how you interact.

Understanding how improvisers do what they do gives us some very clear indications about the conditions required to make a group act more creatively. It gives us, if you like, a little of the grammar for the 'new literacy' of creativity that we require if we are successfully to confront the many challenges we face.

Improv suggests that by becoming more playful, more focused on action and flow, and willing to embrace constraints, you will become a lot more creative. Improv groups show us that in the right conditions, anyone who wants to can make a creative contribution. Which is just as well, given how many contributions are needed.

GAME

OBJECT TAPS

A simple idea-generator game that demonstrates some general principles of brainstorming.

At a glance	Use an everyday object to generate new ideas.
Purpose	Innovation and brainstorming.
Mechanics	People in small teams of five or six. Each with an everyday object and a flip chart.
Set-up	Ask people to list all the qualities of the object, what it can be used for, functions, attributes and so on. Then apply these to the thing you need ideas about.
Debrief	Collect and share ideas. Play Incorporations (see later) to find out which ones people think are best.

HOW THE GAME WORKS

Put people in teams of five or six. First get them to agree what it is they want new ideas about. It could literally be a new product or it could be something less tangible, like how they work together.

Give each group an everyday object - a coffee cup, a pencil sharpener, whatever comes to hand. Ask them to list all the qualities and properties of the object that they can think of - hard, round, white, shiny, etc. Get them to include how it gets used in their list as well (e.g. 'it holds liquid', 'you can use it to trap a wasp'). When they have a good list, which should only take a few minutes, you then invite them to apply things on the list to the thing they want ideas about, by asking 'what if' or 'how could' our thing be round, or hard, or white, etc.? There is a leap involved - you aren't asking these questions literally, but using them to spark off new ideas and insights. For example, imagine you are a consultancy and want ideas about how to find new clients. Thinking and asking about 'round' might lead you to say, 'How about we hold round tables bringing together existing clients to explore what they think our strengths and weaknesses are?' Get them to write down their ideas and choose the two or three they find most interesting.

THINGS TO WATCH OUT FOR

When they start it can help to have them really study the object for a few minutes so that they pay attention to the details in a way they might normally not. Have them pick it up as well so that they notice and include texture, weight, feel and so on. This technique illustrates the importance of structure and stimulus in creativity. You don't come up with new ideas in a vacuum, despite all that enthusiasm for 'blue sky thinking'. Normally new ideas occur by combining and connecting things in new ways, as this game very obviously does. If you understand that general principle you will think of new ways to combine and connect ideas. For example, use a person instead of an object to get your list of qualities - either a real person or a historical figure.

DEBRIEF

Once each team has their top ideas you can read them out and, if you want, get them to organise into groups around the ideas. Write each idea on a sheet of paper, and place it on the floor and have people go and stand next to the one they are drawn to, for example (this is a version of another game, called Incorporations which you will find more detail about in Chapter 7).

This is an adaptation of a game we saw on 'Who's Line is it Anyway?', so the credit really goes to Gary Hirsch.

5
Leadership

If an alien were to land in the middle of an improv performance and say, 'Take me to your leader,' the actors would be stuck. Even if they were cool enough to deal with the appearance of little green men on stage speaking English and spouting Hollywood clichés, the request to identify a leader would floor them.

In improvisation, there is no designated leader. There is no Commander, CEO or President. No head honcho, top dog, big cheese or padrone. So what can improvisation possibly tell us about leadership?

As you might expect, I am going to suggest that the answer is 'plenty'. The reason is that you don't need leaders for there to be leadership. A formal position in the hierarchy, with a corner office, flashy car and big title, guarantees nothing. We have all worked for people who have the position (and the trappings that go with it) but display no leadership. Who knows, we may even have been these people. As Professor Kurt April of Cape Town University puts it: 'I have met many CEOs that I wouldn't follow to the toilet. And many people on the shop floor that I would give my life for.' What we are interested in here is leader*ship*. That elusive ability, wherever it comes from and whoever displays it, to inspire and move people to do things they wouldn't otherwise be willing or able to do.

Improvisers routinely display that ability. They perform under pressure. They are exposed and highly visible. They have to cope with uncertainty and rapid, unpredictable change. They have to interact with the ideas of other people. These are all leadership behaviours and improvisers are rather good at them.

It is the behaviour of leadership that we are going to focus on in this chapter. We will look at what it is that improvisers do that we can learn from or emulate, in order to develop our own leadership capabilities in organisations, or in everyday life.

As our little green man discovered, on the improv stage, there is no single leader. This is the first thing we can learn from improvisers - that leadership can be something everyone does, whatever their formal position. You don't have to wait until you get promoted, you can start now. On stage it has to be this way. The characters that actors play emerge from the action itself, so no one is put in charge. Everyone must actively participate so that ideas come from all quarters; no single perspective is enough. The success of the whole depends upon connecting these different contributions in a coherent way. Everyone is responsible for creating the conditions where the work gets done; no one can do it on their own.

Improvisers display an enviable flexibility because they have such a fluid approach to leadership. Different people have to be able to lead, at different moments, as the situation demands. People must be willing to step up, or step back, as the circumstances require. This means paying close attention and being highly sensitive to what is needed. It also means being willing to let go of your own agenda and ego. Not only does everyone have an *opportunity* to lead, but if the group is to fulfil its potential everyone has the *obligation* to lead, when required.

This isn't unique to the stage. I once had a former soldier in a workshop. He observed, wryly, that in combat 'the person leading is the person who can see best'. The same idea is in play in the famous Toyota Production System where any worker can stop the line. Every individual, at whatever level, is given the chance to lead and the power to exercise it. The person who sees best, leads.

If this is an advantage in manufacturing, in a knowledge business it is vital. There is more information than anyone can absorb, so you need to be able to take advantage of many points of view. If leadership is concentrated in one individual, or even a few, you become vulnerable.

Another military example serves as a striking illustration of this. Within days of the D-Day landings in June 1944 American officers were wearing their helmets back to front. This was not bravado, it was to hide the white lines that officers had on their helmets. The Germans had quickly learned that without officers the American troops didn't know what to do, so they issued orders to target the officers, who as a result took very high casualties. The American officers realised what was happening and started to wear their helmets backwards, so the white stripes didn't show. This shows how concentrating leadership in a few critical nodes (the officers) made the system as a whole more vulnerable to shocks. Turning their helmets around was a logical step, but what the Americans really needed to do was develop more distributed leadership.

Resilience matters. In an interconnected world, shocks, in 1001 forms, from epidemics to economic crises, will abound. We do not know where or when they will occur. They are beyond the ability of even the best informed or most intelligent to predict. Faced with complexity, we don't need better predictions, we need more resilient systems and that means embracing the idea of distributed leadership.

This is a challenge. The idea of distributed leadership is disappointing or threatening to anyone, little green man or otherwise, who believes that a select group ought to have a monopoly on leadership. Unfortunately, one way or another, that means most of us. The figure of the heroic leader is a powerful and widespread idea that has acquired the status of a myth. It suits wannabe heroes because it makes them feel important. It suits the rest of us because it allows us to duck responsibility.

Looking at leadership from the improviser's perspective thus poses some uncomfortable questions. If leadership is lacking, it forces us to look at ourselves and do something about it, rather than lament the shortcomings of others. 'Well, I've done my bit,' is not enough. We must ask what is our own contribution and how we might show more leadership ourselves. This means extending your focus beyond yourself. Disappointingly for anyone who wants to be a hero, it is not all about you.

This does not imply that roles don't matter, or that some people don't - by virtue of their position or experience - have more responsibility than others. What it does mean is that no one has a monopoly on leadership and that each of us can make a difference.

You cannot learn to improvise from a book any more than you can learn to swim in a library (which is why, in this book, I put so much emphasis on practice and include some practical exercises). Improvisation is an embodied ability. It draws on the whole person. Physical sensation, space, position and gesture are all important, as well as reason, emotion and intuition. This means that it can only be developed through experience and practice.

Leadership is also a practical not an academic endeavour. Despite the business schools' enthusiasm for leadership, a purely intellectual approach is too narrow. It won't help you to motivate people, or handle uncertainty. Reading about it is different from doing it. Unfortunately, many leaders with impressive experience are quite underwhelming when you hear them try to explain what they do. Being able to do something does not guarantee that you can explain what it is you do either.

This means that if you want to develop your leadership ability, the focus of your efforts must be on your own experience. By all means take ideas from leaders (great and small) and from books (including this one) but make sure you put them into practice for yourself, in your own context, and see how they play out. Only you can find out how they work for you. You must lean into experience, not shy away from it.

This can be unfamiliar and uncomfortable. In the business world, people talk a good deal about making mistakes but in general errors aren't applauded. We are trained to avoid taking risks and rewarded for doing so. Hollywood is a great example of this ambivalence - it claims to be all about creativity, but in fact is deeply conservative. As a Hollywood insider said to me once, 'Everybody here wants to be the first to do something for the second time.' Such attitudes are widespread. Improvisers, by contrast, are both braver and more philosophical. They accept that discomfort is a necessary part of what they do and embrace it gracefully, instead of ignoring it, wishing it away or struggling against it. When I asked one performer how they dealt with being in such a highly exposed position he said, 'You learn to get comfortable, being uncomfortable.' Wise words indeed.

We would do well to develop the same wisdom in our approach to leadership. Rather than reaching for answers or becoming paralysed by the fear of making mistakes we should accept the discomfort that comes with the territory and learn to become comfortable, being uncomfortable.

One source of comfort is the very idea of practice itself. Faced with an infinite and unpredictable set of possibilities improvisers do not plan or theorise. Instead, their response is to adopt a certain mindset. This is a very open-minded, all-inclusive attitude where no thing is too small to be worthy of notice and everything can be useful. They are magpies. This is an extremely practical attitude and one whose focus is on getting things moving.

With such a practical emphasis it is not surprising that the improvisers' method is based on practice. Through experience and experiment, on stage and in workshops, they have looked for deep, unifying patterns. Based on this experience they have developed a repertoire of behaviours, or practices, that stimulate, frame and channel how you respond.

Thinking of leadership in terms of practice, in the way that improvisers do, is a gift. But just as 'practice' is a noun, 'practise' is a verb, and carries, built into it, the idea of an activity which is continuous and never-ending. A practice is something you do and keep doing. No matter how accomplished you become, you keep at it. The notion of a practice thus cultivates persistence.

This endless demand means that, taken to heart, the idea of practice can be a very ambitious one. Nonetheless, it is also realistic - by accepting that we need to practise, we acknowledge that we do not have the answers. Which means that when setbacks occur we do not lose heart. Having a practice makes it much easier to act in the midst of difficulty. We may get confused, but we don't get derailed. We become 'comfortable, being uncomfortable', as it were.

A practice-based approach moves us away from unattainable ideals of perfection or fixed goals and allows us to become more compassionate, particularly to ourselves. The emphasis shifts from trying to avoid mistakes, to learning from them. Instead of 'Is it right?' we start to ask 'Does it help?' Framing leadership as a practice also starts to erode the unhelpful notion that it is an innate ability. It can't be, or we wouldn't be able to practise it.

So what does it look like to have a practice? Imagine you are lost or stuck. You face a leadership dilemma and don't know whether to go on or go back (either literally, or metaphorically). There is plenty of doubt and uncertainty. The pressure is building and you need to act. In such circumstances there is a risk that you will fall back on familiar responses, such as blame or denial. Most often we simply work harder, as if effort were the answer to every predicament. These responses come all too easily, particularly when we are under stress.

In these circumstances a practice acts as a discipline that guides you. The improv practice gives you three basic questions (or some variation of them) that you can productively ask, namely:

1 How can I notice more? (this will slow you down, help you see things or people you are missing, encourage you to lean into your senses and help you become present, etc.)

2 What can I let go of? (this will encourage you to notice and question assumptions, expectations, invisible rules or personal agendas)

3 How can I use everything? (this will enable you to re-frame problems and errors as opportunities)

Developing the habit of asking these (or similar) questions gives your mind somewhere to go, other than into a spin, especially when you are under pressure, or people are looking to you for guidance. It centres and calms you. It suggests how you might usefully direct your attention and what to look for. These simple steps are always useful and can be repeated endlessly. Whatever other ideas or theories you choose to play with, this practice gives you something immediate to do - it is an obvious place to start when you are stuck or stymied.

This is how the idea of practice is useful. It acts as a compass to help you navigate the inevitable discomfort. It won't make the danger disappear, but it can help you find your way through it.

Great leaders have presence. They make the people they are leading feel seen and heard. This is vital. People need to feel that they matter.

Improvisers develop presence by paying attention. This is part of the practice of 'noticing more'. Whatever your natural skills, you can always listen better or attend more closely to the people around you. This has eternal value because it is an act of generosity - you give of yourself when you pay proper attention to someone. Quite literally, you 'devote' your attention to them and people feel this, which makes them much more inclined to follow you.

A mark of a great leader is someone who, however important they may be, still pays attention to others. Stories abound of leaders like Mandela or Clinton who are inspirational in this respect. This isn't complicated. Yet masters like Mandela can elevate it to the level of genius. Such extraordinary levels of attentiveness may be beyond us, but in an age when technology seduces us into a state of 'continuous partial attention', striving to be more present is one of the most important things you can do. Don't be put off by the fact that it sounds dull.

One specific way to work on this is to make an effort to pay more attention to the person you are with than to what you are going to say next. Notice how you plan ahead, second by second, and let that go. If what you were going to say is important enough it will come back again. Meanwhile, the people you are with will notice and appreciate your full attention. Funnily enough, if you pay attention, ideas and opportunities have a way of presenting themselves to you, without you having to scurry around looking for them.

Another productive tactic is to focus on being changed by what you hear. This is a lot more effective than trying to listen 'better' and it is the instruction that improv directors give their actors. It is a way of tricking yourself into a good habit. If you want to demonstrate you have heard, you have to listen, otherwise you don't know how to react. Being visibly altered leaves other people in no doubt that you have listened.

For example, when Commander Mike Abrashoff took over the USS *Benfold* it was a warship with low morale and poor performance. Not knowing what to do, he started by talking to every crew member. What made this more than a PR stunt, and really got the crew's attention, was when Abrashoff visibly started to implement suggestions he was getting. The changes he made (about food, small arms practice or painting the ship) showed that he wasn't just *talking* to them, he was *listening* to them as well. There is nothing more motivating than seeing your words acted upon.

Paying close attention can help you resolve awkward conversations too. One leader we worked with decided that when she had to give people poor performance reviews, rather than focus on how to present the bad news, she would put more effort into paying close attention to the other person. When she did so she found that they would often raise the issue themselves, which made it easier for both of them. This flips our normal instinct, which is to focus on ourselves. It isn't easy, but if you can manage it, it is a lot less work.

Paying attention to people means paying attention to their ideas as well. Improvisers happily take other people's ideas and build on them, which also builds relationships, with other actors and with the audience. This is the 'yes, and ...' spirit that is at the core of improv.

Leaders need new ideas. By definition, a leadership challenge is a predicament to which there is no known answer. Or to put the same thing another way, if you know the answer, then what you are doing isn't leadership. This means you need to explore a rich diversity of ideas and possibilities in order to move forward. Since other people will see things you don't and have ideas you won't, you need them to contribute.

Part of this is to model the behaviour you would like to see in others, by offering up your own ideas, even if they seem silly or incomplete, without worrying about how it makes you look. What is more important is to pay attention to and use other people's ideas. This requires humility, but a leader who is willing and able to take ideas from anywhere is strengthened, not weakened.

Leadership is often about connecting what is already there. We see this in storytelling games where, often, all that is needed to make sense of the whole is someone to simply add an 'and' or a 'because'. In such a game leadership consists of serving the story, not yourself, and being willing to add a small piece, which makes a connection. Improvisers value 'connective tissue' highly and this is another tip we can take from them. Finding opportunities to connect ideas and people is a wonderfully simple yet extremely powerful piece of leadership behaviour.

By serving the story, rather than yourself, you generate trust. Psychologist and executive coach Jon Stokes says that the more self-centred you are, the less people trust you. He expresses the level of trust people have in a leader as a formula, like this:

$$\text{Level of trust} = \frac{(\text{competence} + \text{reliability} + \text{integrity})}{\text{self-centredness}}$$

Because it is on the bottom of this equation (technically, it is the divisor), being self-centred has a dramatic effect on how much people trust you. Even being a little self-centred erodes trust a lot. Which means that being seen to serve the story isn't just noble, it is a good leadership strategy.

Noticing more also means paying attention to 'weak signals'. On the improv stage a small detail often develops into the main story. For this to happen, the actors have to notice it, act on it, and be willing to let the story develop in a very different way than they may have anticipated.

In business, new ideas and developments - whether threats or opportunities - often appear from the periphery. A new competitor from a completely different category comes crashing in, or a small-scale technological development turns out to have the potential to transform your business. Developing the ability to perceive these weak signals is a fantastic leadership behaviour. Make sure that you pay attention to people and ideas that lie outside the mainstream, in forgotten or neglected departments or functions. Noticing the 'weak signals' that lie on the periphery is important, both to alert you to growing threats and to help you find new opportunities.

Many years ago I met Gene Kranz, the flight controller on Apollo XIII (Gene was the character played by Ed Harris in the movie). Partway through the journey to the moon, there was an explosion of some kind on board the spacecraft. Despite having no idea of the cause, or the extent of the damage, Kranz and his team in Houston had to make certain critical decisions with the eyes of the world upon them. Kranz talked about what to do when uncertainty prevails. 'You have to act before all the data is in,' he said. 'If you wait you would never actually get all the data, because you would lose the spacecraft.' In the face of uncertainty, you must act. This requires courage and, as Kranz explained, a willingness to trust weak or diffuse data - otherwise known as intuition, or hunch.

Improvisers become very practised at acting 'before all the data is in'. They focus on getting going, rather than getting it right. In a situation where you don't know what an answer might look like, this makes a lot of sense. Once you get going you get feedback. You can then adjust or change accordingly. Try nothing and you are none the wiser. Momentum is also motivating.

Putting the emphasis on getting going doesn't mean that you don't care where you go. As a friend of mine is fond of pointing out, 'When you shoot from the hip, you still aim.' My favourite metaphor here is that of a boat. Unless you are moving forward through the water you are at the mercy of wind and tide. Get going and you can steer.

However, when I say this in workshops, people often protest. 'How can I start before I know what's going on?' they ask. It is a deeply ingrained habit. Leadership dilemmas, however, always involve unknowns. The mistake is to assume that because you don't know everything you can't act. Hunch is not the same as no data, it is just data that is below the threshold of conscious rational thought.

Through practice improvisers develop a sense and feel for which offer to accept in order to get moving. Learning to read subtle patterns, including your own feelings and responses, is a skill that can be developed. Improvisers do it all the time, as indeed do many senior business leaders, who use hunch and intuition more than is often supposed (for example Sir John Templeton, financier and founder of Templeton College, Oxford, would often make significant investment decisions based on feel, rather than on concrete reasons).

There is plenty to practise here. We have to let go of our attachment to certainty, particularly in the form of rational knowledge. Forget the idea of anything being 'future-proof'. We need to understand and accept that valid information shows up in many ways - such as sense or intuition - not just in numerical data. We need to develop our sensitivity, or ability to read these diffuse signals, and we need to be willing to act upon them, notice what happens and adjust or change as a result. That should keep you busy.

In nature, all waste is food. There is nothing that isn't

useful to somebody else. Just ask a dung beetle. What a wonderful trick that is. Improvisation's very own version of this elegant ecological truth is that everything is an offer.

Take that idea into the leadership realm and you create a different climate immediately. It is an incredibly constructive way to re-frame problems, errors and failings. Whatever it is, it isn't a problem, it's an offer. Putting the focus on looking for offers is contagious. Good leaders do it instinctively. When Thomas Edison's disheartened foreman reported to his boss that they had tried a thousand different materials for the filament of a light bulb with no success, Edison retorted that this wasn't failure - they now knew a thousand materials that didn't work and they could use this knowledge to help them find one that did.

There is a physical practice that helps with this, which improvisers call being 'fit and well' (rather than 'sick and feeble'). It means being upright, balanced, open, grounded and relaxed, physically, in the face of difficulty and uncertainty. This is the physical embodiment of the practice of seeing everything as an offer, and is in itself very empowering. You can start in your body. Adopt this physical attitude and you become more likely to be able to deal with the difficulty.

Ingvar Kamprad (of the chicken feathers) is another natural. One IKEA manager told me a story about a time when they ordered too many wardrobes. Ten thousand too many. Everyone was nervous about telling Kamprad, but when they did so he was delighted and immediately engaged with the question of what to do with ten thousand wardrobes as an exciting challenge. His attitude seems to have rubbed off throughout IKEA, whose willingness to see everything as an offer allows them to end up selling cardboard roof racks or opening up their warehouse to customers. Enabling people to see mistakes, problems and errors as offers is a very constructive piece of behaviour that creates a positive climate.

Unsurprisingly, this 'keystone' practice is of enormous value in leadership. It is also, for example, a brilliant way for a leader to work with people's objections. In some way or other, leadership involves change of some kind and there will always be objections to this change. Normally these are seen as obstacles or barriers and, far too often, we take against the people that raise them. It becomes personal.

It is much more productive to see objections as offers too. One successful innovator from a large and very conservative company said that whenever someone said no to him (which they did, frequently) he just interpreted it as a request for more information.

Alfred Sloan, CEO of General Motors in its heyday, would adjourn board meetings where he thought everyone had agreed too easily 'in order to generate some constructive disagreement'. He was worried that people were just telling him what they thought he wanted to hear and was wise enough to know that opposing opinions were vital to the health of the organisation, so he encouraged them.

They say that you can tell the quality of an organisation by the speed with which bad news travels upwards. If you see objections or opposing opinions as offers, then you can improve the quality of your organisation at a stroke. Doing so enables you to understand other points of view, show up gaps in your knowledge, or simply give you a read on how people are reacting.

Being willing to see objections as offers is a way to generate constructive dissent, rather than the destructive consent that prevails when people aren't willing to speak up against those in positions of power.

When people interact, they are constantly adjusting their position relative to each other. This is going on all the time, quite naturally, and is independent of your formal position (which is fixed). A child can comfort a parent. A duke may ask his butler for advice. Improvisers call this flexible position 'status'. Your status, in this sense, depends upon your behaviour in the moment. It can shift up or down very quickly.

Improvisers use this understanding to help them create scenes that are credible and engaging. This constant ebb and flow of status is a natural part of human interaction. Understanding this helps develop characters that are realistic enough to engage an audience without the need for a script.

For anyone interested in leadership, understanding that status is flexible, and separate from position, is a profound insight. It lays bare one of the fundamental dynamics of relationships and gives you a whole new dimension to work with. Whatever position you are in, you can play high or low as circumstances demand and shift instantly. This gives you a way to be sensitive and flexible, to modulate your behaviour, to act according to the context, rather than letting your role dictate how you should act. It is therefore much easier to be authentic.

Simply understanding that status is always in play is valuable in itself. But we can go further. Improvisers can tell you what to do to shift your status up or down. The practice can give us an understanding of the benefits of high and low and, perhaps most importantly, make visible how we often confuse status and position.

To play high, or raise your status, you can:

— be definitive ('there are two important points here')

— invoke authority ('I saw in the *Financial Times* ...')
— draw on exclusive experience ('when we started the business ...')

There are certain physical cues that raise status automatically: speaking in an even, measured tone, pushing your chest out and, curiously enough, holding your head still while talking (if you don't believe me, try it!) This isn't a comprehensive list, but you get the idea.

To play low, or lower your status, you can:

— be self-deprecating ('I know a little about this')
— express doubt or uncertainty ('I am not sure what this means')
— elevate others ('John is the one who really understands Nigeria')

Physically, you lower your status by moving or fidgeting, fluctuating the speed and volume at which you speak, or by adopting a lower position than someone else (e.g. sit in a lower chair). Again, there's more but this captures the gist of it.

People normally assume that a leader has to play high status. This is a mistake. Think about it. How do you feel about people that always act as if they know it all, who are uniformly decisive and determined? Do you warm to them? Do you trust them? Would you willingly offer up your ideas and energy? In short, would you choose to follow them?

In fact, playing high status has plenty of downsides; we just tend to ignore them. High status distances you from people. It is exclusive, in the negative sense. It is not engaging, nor does it encourage people to take initiative. It can be intimidating. However impressive it may make them appear, someone that relentlessly plays high status will pay a price for that inflexibility.

Low status, on the other hand, has advantages, which we also tend to miss. It breaks down barriers, generates empathy, defuses tension and can be very charming. It is inclusive not exclusive. In an era when collaboration and creativity are of increasing importance, when complexity means that we face more unknowns and faster changes, these are important qualities for a leader to cultivate. Of course, low status in excess can appear weak, but a complete absence of low status actually makes you *more* vulnerable, not less.

Thus the improviser's understanding of status offers two extremely useful lessons for the practice of leadership. First, by pointing out that there is a dynamic element in how we position ourselves relative to other people, it opens up a whole new dimension for us to work with. We need not be taken prisoner by our position. On occasion, junior people can play high status and senior people can play low status to good effect.

Secondly, it gives us a palette of possibilities that we can learn to use skilfully and sensitively, according to the particular circumstances. High and low status both have advantages and disadvantages. If you understand these, whatever formal position you occupy, you can practise raising or lowering your status from moment to moment according to what you feel is required at that moment. This invites you to be playful with status, rather than feeling you are bound by it. It allows you to try different ways of acting and see what happens as a result. Which, in turn, helps you not to take things (or yourself) too seriously.

The ability to flex and adapt is absolutely central to the work of leadership. Harvard Professor Ronald Heifetz, one of the world's most respected leadership thinkers, says, 'Leadership is an improvisational art. You may have an overarching vision, clear, orienting values, and even a strategic plan, but what you actually do from moment to moment cannot be scripted.'

Improvisers have a lot to offer us when it comes to the moment-to-moment business of what we actually do. They show us that leadership is not the special preserve of elites, but an ongoing practice we can all engage in. They offer us a few simple ideas, like listening and seeing things as offers, that may not seem very grand, but which, in fact, go to the very heart of leadership. They also invite us, through an understanding of status, to develop a more sophisticated and flexible way of relating to the people we are endeavouring to lead.

This is both a mighty relief and a mighty challenge. The work we must do to develop our leadership is actually very simple. We do not have to know the answers or become a hero. Which is good news.

Instead, we can focus our efforts on some very simple behaviours that will help increase our capacity to respond creatively and effectively to uncertainty and change. This is a never-ending practice that challenges many of the assumptions and beliefs we hold about leadership. That is the challenge.

GAME

SWEDISH STORY

It may help to see this game before you play it. You can watch a version of it in my Do Lecture at:
www.thedolectures.com/speakers/robert-poynton

At a glance	A storyteller has to incorporate random words into a story.
Purpose	Learning to use blocks, barriers and obstacles as offers whilst continuing to pursue a goal. Understanding that if you see something as an offer it becomes one and there is nothing you can't use.
Mechanics	Play in pairs. Swap roles and play again.
Set-up	Demo. Then put people in pairs, get them to allocate roles and give them a title. Call time then swap them over.
Debrief	What did you expect? How did the experience change that? How did you, as storyteller, feel about the words? How easy was it to give words that didn't fit? How is this dynamic similar to work?

HOW THE GAME WORKS

The basic dynamic is that one person tells a story and a second person shouts out words that the storyteller has to use. It isn't a memory test, so the word-giver can only give a second word once the first one has been used, but as soon as it has been, he or she can give another one. The additional wrinkle is that the word-giver is invited to choose words that have absolutely nothing to do with the story.

Having demonstrated the dynamic you then invite them to play. They will be aghast (thinking 'I can't possibly do that') but don't worry about that. Reassure them that they won't be performing but all playing at the same time. That will calm them down a bit. Not a lot, but a bit. Carry on anyway. Get them into pairs and ask them to decide who will be the storyteller and who will be the word-giver. If they dither, tell them they will each have a turn, so it doesn't matter who starts. Or just instruct them that the taller of the two will be storyteller first (they will always find a taller one, even if they are very similar heights). Before they start, invite them to consider which role they think will be easier.

Then give them a title. The same for everyone. To generate this, just look around the room and use something you can see. Reassure them that their story need not be long. Then, off they go. Let the stories run for a bit and when you think they are running out of steam shout above the hubbub, 'Find an end if you can,' then 'Last word,' and finally 'Stop, wherever you are.' Swap them over. Give them a new title and repeat.

THINGS TO WATCH OUT FOR

People recognise the dynamic in this game from real life. Ask them and they will very quickly make the connection because at work people are always having to adapt to things that come at them unexpectedly. Leaders in particular have to set and keep to a direction whilst overcoming all sorts of obstacles. If you want to coach people, invite them not to use the title immediately (people often do this automatically). Saving the title can help you find an end to your story. It is easier to work your way towards something. Point out that they don't always have to use the words immediately either. The words you are given aren't under your control but you can choose when and how you use them, so you have more influence than you might think. Sometimes it works well to hold the word for a little; on other occasions, just say it, then work out how to justify it in

the story by back-filling. As the group play watch the body
language. Eavesdrop on their stories.

DEBRIEF

Ask who is leading this exercise. On the one hand the storyteller has to pursue a goal (or vision) and adapt to things
coming at them. So they have to maintain direction and adapt.
On the other hand, the word-giver can give input or direction
via the words, but cannot control the story. You can explore
the two roles as a way of looking at elements of leadership
behaviour. How did the storyteller keep on track? What role did
the frequency and kind of words have? How did they influence
the direction of the story? I would argue that leadership isn't
in the roles here, but in the behaviour of adapting under stress
and using disparate inputs.

Ask them how the experience compared with their expectation.
Which role did they think was going to be harder? Which one
was actually harder? How did the expectation differ from
the experience? Normally they overestimate the difficulty
of incorporating the words and underestimate the difficulty
of giving the words. We tend to assume that visible effort is
what really counts. Which isn't necessarily true. Ask about
the feelings you have as storyteller towards the words? Did
they help or hinder? How would you have found it without the
words? Ask about the word-giver role. What was hard there?
People often get sucked into the story and actually find it very
difficult to give words that don't connect (a warning of how
easily groupthink can occur).

WHEN TO USE SWEDISH STORY

You can use a demonstration of Swedish Story to impress people
because it looks a lot more difficult than it is. Or you might want
to entertain them, or to demonstrate how improvisers create
something in real time overcoming obstacles. This makes it very

useful at the beginning of workshops in particular.

To do a demo you need a volunteer (or a colleague) to give the words. Make sure they are clear about their role and that they understand they can give a second word as soon as the first one is used. The only thing they can really do that will upset the demonstration is to freeze and forget to give words, leaving you completely on your own. If they do, pause the story and remind them of their role, then carry on. If they do the opposite and give you a torrent of words one after another, remember, until you use each word they are barred from giving you another one. So, hold off using a word while you progress your story a bit and they will have to wait. You can invite the audience to observe themselves as they watch a demonstration. This allows you to explore what engages an audience, so you can get value from it even if you don't have them play it (that way you also don't blow the gaff about how easy it is, so they continue to be impressed).

I find it particularly useful to demonstrate that offers don't all come gift-wrapped, which makes it a good follow-on from 'Presents'. This game demonstrates that with the right attitude, anything, however negative, can still be reframed as an offer. This is very empowering. It would also be a useful thing to do if you and your team face a task that seems impossible. Have them try this to show them that they can do things they don't think they are capable of.

People often ask why it is called Swedish Story. I have no idea why it was called this, but a participant in a workshop once offered a brilliant, if invented, explanation. 'It's like going to IKEA,' he said. 'You end up with all sorts of stuff you didn't want or ask for.'

Gary learned this one from Randy Dixon, Creative Director of Unexpected Productions in Seattle.

6
Improv in Action

I would like to make a confession. I am not very interested in improvisational theatre. I am not trained in improv. I do not perform on stage and I have no ambition to do so. My interest is not in the theatre. It is in the improvisation.

Improvisation is what life does. Nothing living, from a bacterium to a blue whale, has a script for their life. This includes you. Somehow or other, every living being copes with untold complexity without a plan, and always has.

What improv theatre gives you is a way to get to grips with this. It is like a laboratory in which to study how improvisation works and thus, in a sense, how life works. It makes the underlying dynamics simple and visible. There are games to play, a language you can learn and tools to apply.

I hope that in these pages you will have found some ideas that enable you to perform better. Techniques that make your presentations, conversations and meetings more effective and more enjoyable. Practices that help you to think better on your feet and become more responsive, flexible and creative. At the same time, I would like to suggest that this is not all we have to learn from an understanding of improvisation. There is more in play here than a few neat tricks to engage an audience or brainstorm new ideas. It has a relevance that goes beyond the stage or stage-like.

Improvisation demonstrates that you can have order without control (just like nature does). This is a radical thought. It goes counter to almost everything we have been taught. It means that you don't necessarily need to work so hard, or get so stressed, trying to organise, plan or control everything. You don't always have to break things down into little pieces and analyse what is going on. There are other options.

Unfortunately, this is hard to see, because the analytical approach has become such a dominant narrative. It is so deeply woven into the way we think and talk that we forget it is one approach among many. We mistake a truth for *the* truth. Yet any one way of thinking is always partial, limited and prejudiced. No single lens will enable you to see everything. Science has just as much potential for fundamentalism as any religion. It gives us a great deal, but not without cost. When we treat life as a form of machinery, it isn't surprising that we end up stressing ourselves and damaging living systems.

We forget that analysis and planning is a very recent human invention. Our amazing mental abilities have catapulted us an enormous distance in a short space of time (which perhaps explains why we are so disorientated). Nonetheless, however clever we are, our plans cannot capture the fundamental nature of things, or of ourselves. No amount of cleverness can.

Our analysis leaves out the irregular bits. The misfits. The outliers. The mess. Anything that cannot be controlled is, by definition, excluded from a randomised controlled trial. The emotions which drive us are omitted from the calculation of rational self-interest that we lay so much store by. The trouble is that the mess - that unruly, complex, fluid bundle of interconnections - is where we all live.

Thus embracing a more improvisational way of being means un-learning some old habits, as well as learning some new ones.

One of these is our enthusiasm for seeing things as either/or, not 'yes, and ...' The desire to divide things into two opposing categories is strong and starts early. In the West, we are brought up this way. At my school, aged 16, everyone had to choose either arts or science. I wanted to do both. I was told this was impossible. It wasn't, but the staff were so attached to the categories they had invented that they could not see any other possibility. Even the pupils joined in, by tidily sorting themselves into groups of their own, which were equally separate. You were either sporty or clever. You couldn't be both.

Given this kind of education it is no surprise that people imagine they have to choose between planning or improvisation, that it is either one or the other. Forced with a sharp choice, they automatically plump for planning, and conclude that improvisation isn't relevant to them.

This is a misunderstanding. Improvisation is not an alternative to analysis and planning. It is a complement. You need both. You cannot run everything by improvising, but you cannot run anything without it. Take building for example. You can't build without a plan, but you have to be able to adapt creatively along the way or you will never finish, let alone get a good result. This is true whether you are extending the kitchen, or building an Olympic Stadium. We spent two years building our house and I was staggered by the amount of improvisation that had to be done on site by the craftsmen to correct mistakes, oversights or missed opportunities in the plan. Many of the most distinctive and most pleasing features of the final building - like the porch, the cellar or the garage - weren't on the plans at all. They emerged from the work itself.

Journeys are another perfect example. If I were to ask you to tell me a story of a wonderful trip or journey, I would bet good money that it will include some element of unexpectedness or improvisation. You are unlikely to tell me the story of something that went exactly to plan. This doesn't mean you shouldn't plan your holiday, but be prepared to adapt and change to what happens along the way or you run the risk of missing out. I once accepted an offer to hop a ride on a truck across the salt flats at Uyuni in Bolivia at ten minutes' notice. My plan had me heading in another direction altogether. Had I followed it, I would have missed walking across the border to Chile under the most incredible stars I have ever seen, or bathing in a hot spring while condors flew overhead.

Another of the deeply ingrained habits that improvisation challenges is our enthusiasm for taking things to pieces. For an improviser there is too much information and too little time to do that. They learn to work with sense and feel, which are faster. Their instinct is to join things up, which is how they create the ideas and actions that drive their stories forward. One great way to join things up, which has worked amazingly for me, is to connect people together. I can't count the number of times that acting on a hunch like this has led to a new friendship, opportunity or adventure.

Taking an engine to pieces is a good way to understand it. Taking a person to pieces in order to understand them isn't. Yet we do it all the time, without even noticing what is lost in the process. The psychology I studied at university reduced what I felt about a piece of music, or a girl, to a sequence of cells firing. I am sure lots of cells were firing (especially when Mary Banks floated across the lawn) but life, as we experience it, is more than that.

Improvisation teaches you to build things up, not break them down. Think about this when you next re-organise (you probably won't have to wait very long). What is it that matters most - how the bits fit together on the org chart, or whether people feel connected to each other? I know people that write a spreadsheet to analyse which house they might buy. That might work as post rationalisation but it won't help you find the house you love. Instead of trying to understand the bits, focus on the whole. You can practise this by choosing quickly in restaurants. Don't analyse the dishes, choose on feel. You will waste less time, enjoy your food more and get practised at making more improvisational decisions.

At the heart of improvisation is a fundamentally different attitude to control. As we have seen, improvisers create stories and ideas through simple, repeated behaviours, like noticing and connecting. This is where they put their energy. This is in stark contrast to a business like advertising, even though it is supposed to be a creative business. When I worked in advertising the most interesting ideas we came up with occurred *in spite* of how things were organised, not because of them. There is a lot of talk about 'thinking out of the box' but creativity is, in fact, boxed in. People want to own it. Even now, clients ask me what the deliverables are from a creativity course, with no intended irony.

It is an awful lot easier to get ideas from improvisers than it is from an advertising agency. They are far more fluent, and therefore far more effective, because they are willing to go where the journey takes them. If you really want to become more creative, you will need to learn to do the same. Let go of wanting to know, in advance, precisely what you are going to get. It is easier that way, as well as more effective. Imagine you come home from work exhausted and there, teeming with energy, is a toddler, eager to play. Instead of feeling you have to invent something clever, just start to play and see what emerges. I remember an occasion with my eldest son, who was then about two, where I just worked with what he gave me. He gave me a ball, so I threw it. He brought it back so I threw it somewhere else and it quite quickly became an intricate game of deception and deceit. We created this game without deciding anything in advance. And my two year old did most of the work.

The genius of improvisation is that it embodies a mindset which offers a counterpoint to the dominant narrative.

There are things we have to give up in order to embrace it, but in return it gives us a different way to see things and a different way to act, which will help us in ways we can't possibly predict. It enables us to enjoy, rather than endure, the uncertain and the unpredictable. It invites us to engage in a different way - less push, more pause.

Which is not to say that improvisation is the answer. But it is a healthy response to a world that is beyond your control. Complexity demands an improvised response.

———————

Fifteen years after blundering across improv, I am as interested in this work as I ever have been. Which even I find surprising. It is, of course, great fun getting paid to play, but I don't think that is why I do it. I think it is because I keep learning.

There is continuous learning on a small scale. I discover new games, or variations, or new ways to apply the ones I already know. I learn from colleagues and clients who use things in ways I would never imagine. Participants in workshops make new observations, which lead to new conversations. I get to work with different kinds of people - from accountants to Zen monks, including African politicians, Brussels' bureaucrats, investment bankers or primary school teachers. All of which is great.

But what really keeps me interested are the big leaps. Every now and then something happens, apparently by chance, that sparks off a cascade of connections and insights I could never have anticipated. It is a glorious feeling.

The first of these was when I met Gary Hirsch, in Portland, Oregon. We met to talk about his art, but he happened to make a few passing comments about improv. Odd though it may seem, in an instant I connected what he was saying to complexity theory. I had been studying the science of complexity and adaptive systems for years, because I felt it held great promise for changing the way we think about organisations and creativity. The trouble was I couldn't explain it for toffee. Improv, by contrast, was something I could use. A business, a great friendship and everything else I have written about followed.

Another of these leaps occurred when I realised that the leadership programme I had worked on for years at Oxford could itself be seen as a piece of improvisation. This made sense of a wealth of past experience and helped inform the efforts of the people leading it. I am still working with (and learning from) this insight today.

What makes me excited about the future, however, is a leap that I owe to a complete stranger I met at the

Copenhagen Jazz Festival in the summer of 2011. I was at one of the open-air concerts which fill parks and squares throughout the city when I fell into conversation with a South African software engineer. Since we were listening to jazz improvisation, I mentioned that I worked with improv theatre and my companion asked if I was familiar with 'Agile Project Management' and 'SCRUM'. When I told him I wasn't he started to explain them, with great enthusiasm.

What he described were ways of working where many strands of 'notice more, let go and use everything' had been woven into the process itself. Teams would review progress every day. Roles weren't prescribed. People worked on what they had energy for. The structure was designed to provoke quick responses and new combinations, not exercise control. Thus improvisational behaviour was stitched into the very fabric of the way things were organised, on purpose, in advance.

I listened, amazed. It was thrilling to discover that so many of the ideas that I work with had been embraced and integrated so elegantly by software engineers. More importantly, it dawned on me that for over ten years, I had only been seeing part of the picture. It felt like I had discovered a door to a garden I didn't know was there.

I realised that with my consultancy, On Your Feet, I had been working at the level of behaviour. We tried to give people an experience that would help them see, understand and apply the practices of improvisation so they could become more flexible, adaptable and creative themselves. We would apply this learning to their problem or organisation, but we would start with behaviour and build up from there.

The stranger in Copenhagen helped me see that this isn't the only place to plug these ideas in. What we had

been doing wasn't wrong, but there was a very obvious
'yes, and ...' that we hadn't seen. You could also start, like
the Agile Project people, with the organisation. You could
design a process to promote, encourage and reward agile,
improvisational behaviour. Hard-wire in a daily meeting
and people have no choice but to iterate fast.

This opened up a whole new territory. If you
consciously held the improv practices in mind at the
outset how would you design the systems and processes
of the organisation differently? How would you change
team composition? Timelines? Review processes? New
product development? Decision making? Remuneration?
If you wanted to make sure people were present, listening,
accepting more and blocking less, what implications would
this have for the structure? Plenty, I am sure.

Though this was new it also felt familiar. Improv itself
has structures that help people behave in a way that
generates a rich stream of creative output - we call them
games.

Building improv practices into the design of an organisation
would have a couple of advantages. First, you wouldn't
need to rely on individual learning. People are used to
following rules, so if you give them different rules you will
generate different behaviour. Careful design of those rules
could promote accepting offers, being present, and so on.
Make these the operating system and people will adopt the
practices without even realising it is what they are doing.
This is why improv games work with novices. The rules of
the game generate the behaviour required.

The second advantage is that people wouldn't have to
fight the existing structure. People's efforts to adopt the
practices of improvisation can flounder in the face of an
organisation that resists (which is why some people find it

easier to apply the learnings in their personal rather than their professional lives).

If you re-design the organisation, or elements of it, to support improv-style behaviour, that difficulty goes away.

As I reflected on this I realised that this already happens and not just in Agile Project Management. There were plenty more examples of precisely this kind of thing. We are already doing it, we just tend not to notice.

For example, I heard a lovely story about a software company that invited its designers to help each other with their own, personal, projects for a day. These were the things people had personal passion for, not work stuff. This is a good way to use what you have - your people and the ideas they already have energy for.

It was a great piece of letting go too, because they did it with no particular end in mind - just to see what emerged. What did emerge, in fact, were ideas of such quality, with such energy behind them, that they decided to abandon their formal innovation process, which was cumbersome and ineffective by comparison. They institutionalised the improvised method, letting go completely and accepting the new offer, to create a new stream of flow. The net result was better ideas in less time and more motivated staff.

3M have, for decades, given people a time budget to work on their own ideas. Gore Associates (inventors of the famous 'GORE-TEX' fabric) concentrates on the human scale, and creates 'village'-sized wholes, of about 200 people, where roles are fluid and people don't have titles. Semco is a Brazilian engineering company whose structures are all about promoting interaction and autonomy and nothing about control.

Semco sounds unique until you hear about Morning Star. Morning Star is the largest tomato-bottling company in California, yet its employees write their own job descriptions and set their own salaries. Sounds like there isn't much left to let go of.

The Ariel Atom is an incredibly innovative sports car that outperforms a Ferrari, at a fraction of the cost. Its structure is borrowed from an insect (it has an exoskeleton) and it is made of completely standard parts. Jeremy Clarkson says it is the most exhilarating thing he has ever driven. Talk about using what you have.

During a takeover crisis a steel company in Canada adopted three rules for meetings so they could make decisions quickly.

IMPROV IN ACTION

The rules were:
1 The meeting decides.
2 The meeting is whoever is in the room.
3 The door to the room is always open.

That way anyone could participate in the decision making but you had to be there. Presence mattered.

It was ironic that it took the Agile Project Management story to make me realise that you could deliberately design improvisational processes into an organisation, because we had done exactly that with On Your Feet. But then, as we say in Spain, 'in the house of the blacksmith they have wooden knives'.

There are far more of these improvisational stories than we realise for the simple reason that we don't tell them this way. We post-rationalise our success, misrepresenting and misunderstanding it in the process.

For example, Richard Pascale, a leading American business thinker, who I work with at Oxford, tells the story of Honda in America. Their success was hailed as an example of brilliant strategy. Richard, who knew something about Japan, had a hunch this wasn't the whole story. He spent time getting to know the Honda people who had been personally involved when they set up their American operation and discovered that in fact, strategy had not been the most important thing. Like Richard, Honda had acted on hunch and feel. They had made many mistakes and errors along the way - for example, choosing a model because its handlebars 'look like Buddha's eyebrows' didn't show much insight into post-war America. They did not plan in detail. What they were brilliant at was noticing what was happening on the ground and responding quickly. Often, without telling head office. Their success was due to their ability to adapt, which Richard called 'The Honda Effect'. Yet the business schools were trumpeting it as a triumph of strategy.

This isn't surprising. The dominant narrative looks for standard, unifying models not anecdotal stories about maverick companies adapting to particular circumstances. The trouble is, particular circumstances are what we all face. 'Anecdotal' should be a compliment not a criticism. Such stories provide insight and inspiration into how we might design more organic, less mechanical organisations - the organisations of the future.

Improvising is the most natural thing in the world. We all do it. You are doing it now. Your eyes, skin, gut, blood and brain are all improvising, each on their own and altogether. Like a forest, or traffic on our roads, or email traffic on the internet, or the food supply to New York City, the most stupendously complex flows are organised in a wonderfully intricate, improvised dance. There is no one in control.

Understanding this is a fabulous liberation. Taking the few, very simple ideas that improv offers us to heart can fundamentally shift how we go about our everyday lives and work. They help us to accept, with humility, that we play a small part in an incomprehensibly complex world. They enable us to reconnect with our own, irreducible, improvisational nature and, most importantly, give us something practical and simple to do.

7
Game On

Since this is a 'Do' book, I want to close on a practical note, and focus on the doing. To that end I would like to offer you two more 'killer' games, to add to those that have been woven throughout. However, before we get to those, let's give them some context, by taking a step back and making some general observations about what games do and what you can do with them.

Improv games aren't just for fun, nor are they competitions or puzzles. They are a vehicle that creates an experience for participants.

The games work because they encapsulate the practices we have explored in this book. For example, when you play Swedish Story (see page 108) the rules of the game force people to accept. Incorporations (see below) uses physical offers to create connections or give feedback quickly. One to Twenty (also below) forces you to let go of systems and agendas.

What this means is that through playing the games you are introducing people to the practices as well. You may be using them for a specific purpose, like generating new ideas or changing the energy in the room, but at the same time you are working by stealth at a deeper level, giving people an experience of how productive and satisfying it can be to work in an improvisational way. You allow them to discover, through play, a different way to work (even a different way to be).

The fact that the content is remote from the business itself doesn't matter. Sportsmen train using exercises they would never use on the field of play. The same is true here. In a complex world developing tolerance for ambiguity is ever more important. That is hard to do on the job. An improv exercise is one way to develop that capacity, to feel what it is like, to see how you respond, where you are found wanting and where you have surprising ability. The beauty of these games is that, done well, they allow us to notice something about ourselves, and what happens as a result of how we behave. Playful though it may be, this is serious work.

The games I have explained are tried and tested. They work. Nonetheless, there is nothing sacrosanct about them and it follows that you shouldn't treat what I have offered you here with too much respect. Where one game ends and a new one begins is hard to say, and doesn't matter anyway. What matters is the atmosphere it creates and the response people have. Absurdly, some improv groups try to 'own' (even copyright) certain games, which completely misses the point.

So, regard what I have written (or what anyone else you might consult has written) as a start point, not an end. Don't just play the games, play around with them. This is not a recipe, it is a set of ingredients and you are the chef. Add to them, subtract from them, bend them, twist them, adapt them, combine them, steal elements from one and inject them into another. After all, that's how they were invented in the first place. Games are created and evolve through the doing. They are the result of past play, honed through experience, embellished and elaborated by different interpretations, enriched by 'mistakes' and misunderstandings. The games are the product of the practices as well as the embodiment of them.

There are lots of ways to be inventive with games. My favourite way to innovate is when participants make a 'mistake' and instead of correcting them, you use it. What a gift that is. You just have to be prepared to let go of your plan or idea of how the game 'should' work, take whatever people have added and let it run to see what happens. We were once working with a new MBA group (at Portland State University) when someone spontaneously added some extra information that turned a simple name-learning game into a rich, complex story game. It doesn't always work as perfectly as that, but if you share with the group what has happened they will normally join in enthusiastically and make all sorts of suggestions about new things to try. At the very least they will be impressed that you are willing to respond to them in this way, rather than trotting out a prepared piece.

You can find new purposes for these games as well as new rules or variants. Other things you can do include playing around with the set-up, adding your own riffs, finding new debrief questions or more economical ways to explain the rules.

Choosing which games to use and designing workshops is a subtle business. I am still learning myself, after 15 years, but let me give you a few pointers. My aim is to give you enough to get going, so that you can find your own way, rather than trying to follow me. You can use these games in two basic ways - combine them to create a workshop, or use them as 'refreshers' to punctuate a gathering of some kind. I would encourage you to start small. Run a single game either to kick off, conclude or enliven a meeting, for example. Or to keep people occupied during a delay. If that works you can build things up from there. If it doesn't 'work' it would be interesting to think about why that was and what was it that you understood by the game 'working' - which is normally quite a revealing question to ask yourself.

When thinking about which game or games to play, pay attention to the physical surroundings. How much space do you have, how easily can people move around, what furniture is there? Think about your audience requirements as well (remember these, from 'Communication' - Chapter 3). Think about the context. What is the meeting or conference for, what else is going to be happening, how might a game enhance the experience? The size of the group is another basic variable you can use to help you choose which games might work best.

If you get more ambitious and want to run a workshop then I would encourage you to choose a number of games in advance but not stick rigidly to a plan. Prepare a territory not a path. Pay attention to what happens in the room and adapt accordingly. Variation is always good - a loud game followed by a quiet game, a whole group game followed by a pair game. To be rigid about using improvisational exercises is contradictory and will undermine what you are trying to do. If you want to have an impact on people you need to walk the walk.

Part of that walk is understanding that the games are not formulaic. They provide a framework, within which people have an experience. Although there are consistent patterns, that experience can be different every time. You never know how people will respond. Something new can always crop up. They are a rich source of learning precisely because each time you play them, there is a good chance that somebody will see something that you haven't seen before or respond in a way you hadn't anticipated.

This is important. If you play a game in order to prove a particular point, it is a way of trying to control people. If you can't let go of that there is a good chance you will be tripped up and people will interpret things in a quite unexpected way which will derail you. Let people have their own experience, whatever that is. Don't fight this, embrace it. Allow things to emerge and enjoy the fact that people see things in different ways. It keeps you learning and interested in the group, which is a boon for them, as well as for you.

You need to be clear about this because participants won't be. People are used to being given puzzles or problems that they have to solve and they tend to bring that attitude to this experience. I have even seen people trying to work out how to 'win' a game like Presents. Be ready to remind them (frequently) that these games have no answers.

After playing, people will often ask, 'What was the point of that game?' This isn't necessarily aggressive or critical (so don't leap into judgement and presume it is) but it often reveals their assumptions. They frequently want to know what the *right* answer was, i.e. what they were *meant* to take from the game.

How to deal with this could be a book in itself, but obviously, what you want to do is to treat the question as an offer. Do that and even if your questioner really is being cynical or deliberately provocative you will get something to work with. My instinct would be to ask them what *they* think the point was, not as a defence, but out of genuine interest. After all, there is a chance I might learn something new. They might well see something I don't and they might just be dying to say it - which gives you the opportunity to 'see' them massively, which will help engage them (remember the importance of 'seeing' the audience?) Having done this I would then probably share what my purpose was (otherwise it seems like I am being evasive). And at some level, albeit a very open one, I *will* have something to say. This is likely to be something like 'I want to explore the idea of making offers' or 'I want people to move'. This may be very different from the kind of 'point' they had in mind, but we can then explore that difference.

So by all means think carefully about what you want to do and why, but don't get attached to a specific outcome. The same game will work differently on a different day with a different group anyway. Which also makes life much more interesting for you.

Enough talk. Here are a final couple of games for you to play and play around with. Treat them as a starting offer to build on. And from there, 'game on', as it were …

GAME

ONE TO TWENTY

This game can drive some people nuts, particularly those individuals that like to be in control. I think that is probably why I like it so much.

At a glance	A group counts from 1 to 20.
Purpose	To make visible desires for prediction and control. To develop attention and awareness.
Mechanics	People speak single numbers out loud. No systems or gestures. If two people coincide, you go back to the beginning.
Set-up	Set up a circle. Explain. Join in yourself. When you hear two numbers coincide start again by saying 'one'. Point out when people are trying to use systems (e.g. going round the circle, pointing).
Debrief	What happened? Emotionally as well as practically? Were we able to do it without a system? If not, why not?

HOW THE GAME WORKS

The aim is to get a group of people to count from one to twenty, in order, using no gestures or signals and without establishing any kind of system or fixed pattern (like going around the circle in order). If two people say the same number, even if only part of the word overlaps, you go back to one and start again. Anyone can take the group back to one if they hear two people coincide. You should be prepared to join in and make sure this happens, until the group starts to take responsibility themselves.

THINGS TO WATCH OUT FOR

This game shows up how strong our desire to impose a system is. People often try to work out what the 'trick' is by quizzing you endlessly before you start, as if it were some kind of trap. If they do so, suggest that they explore through the doing, which is much more efficient (though far less comfortable for people, which is why they keep asking questions about what is permitted).

Once you start, within a matter of seconds people may try to establish a pattern, by pointing, or using a repeated pattern, or by saying all the numbers themselves. If this occurs, remind them the goal is to do it without imposing a system. This will frustrate some people. If you feel the need to defuse it, you can point out that the game simply emulates real life, where you can't impose your own system of control upon the world. Be aware they might get irritated with you! If they do, don't take it personally (this is a good chance to practise letting go of judgement).

If you want you can let them have their system. If you do, make sure you get them to both notice and reflect on what they are doing in the debrief, because what they have really done is to avoid the task. This means they have a low tolerance for ambiguity and uncertainty, 'negative capability' as poet John Keats called it. In a complex world, that is a capability you really need to develop.

Some groups just don't believe it is possible. If so, call their attention to this and invite them to consider what the effect of this belief is on their performance. This can take you straight into a very fruitful conversation about how our beliefs affect our work. Another common response is to go fast. You can point this out and invite them to try a different rhythm.

Emotion and tension rise quickly in this game, particularly when you get past ten but don't get to twenty, so it is useful to keep track of time. Groups can be incredibly intolerant of what they see as 'failure'. If you can point out to them that they have only been playing for a few minutes, it gives them some perspective and also helps them realise how impatient they can be. In fact it isn't failure, it is just an experience; there is nothing significant at stake and the number twenty is arbitrary - it could just as easily be thirty (indeed, that is one of the variations you can introduce). Only once have I had to give up altogether because the group got so tense, which, funnily enough, was with a group of Zen monks.

DEBRIEF

'What happened?' is really the only question you need here. Along with observations of your own about the specific things that happened (the desire to dominate or control, lack of silence, impatience and so on) that you can point out and explore.

VARIATIONS

If people really struggle and you don't want to abandon the game, lower the target. Make it ten or eight. If they find it easy, you can raise the target. Other variations include looking outwards instead of inwards, closing your eyes, or doing the exercise while walking around. If you wish you can explore the effect of any of these on what happens.

You can also play with no specific target, but with an invitation to get to as high a number as possible. I have worked with groups that have got into the seventies.

WHEN TO USE ONE TO TWENTY

This is a game which raises the question of what you do when you can't control things, which, let's face it, is a lot of the time.

It also gives you an experience of the power of being really present (or the difficulties that can ensue when you aren't).

When you are, a natural rhythm emerges and it becomes quite easy. It also shows the power of *not* acting - it really helps if some people hold back. Which again, can lead to a really interesting conversation about the value of silence, space and emptiness. So I use it when I want to quieten things down. It shows the power of stillness, which is a nice counterpoint to the busyness of most of modern life.

One leadership consultant I work with, Amanda, came up with a brilliant use of this game that is about none of these things. She used the fact that people want to tell others what to do to make it an exercise about giving feedback. She would stop the counting from time to time and invite people to give other individuals feedback about what they were doing and how they felt it was affecting the group's performance. The tension inherent in the game raised the stakes and made these conversations highly charged, which provided great learning for how to have difficult conversations.

This game came from an 'Applied Improvisation Network' conference, though we can't trace who precisely taught it to us. Sorry.

GAME

INCORPORATIONS

A very simple, very flexible physical game good for forming a group, making visible shared interests or getting feedback.

At a glance	A group self-organises into smaller sub-groups based on a question from the facilitator (e.g. 'How are you feeling right now?')
Purpose	To find patterns and connections in the group. A quick way to give feedback on something physically.
Mechanics	People wander around the room talking to others to find the people whose response is similar to their own. Various questions are explored, one after another.
Set-up	People on their feet around the room. Explain and start.
Debrief	Which group is which? How many in each? On what basis did you form the groups?

HOW THE GAME WORKS

First teach them the mechanics by giving a simple instruction like: 'Organise yourselves into groups according to the clothes you are wearing.' There are two things they have to decide in order to do this - first, what are the criteria they are using (colour, cloth, shape, cut?) and then, which group they are in. If they ask you for the criteria, tell them that is part of the task. They have to self-organise, which means moving around the room, talking to each other and sorting themselves into groups.

Encourage them to trawl what else is out there and not just find a way of fitting into the first group they meet. Once they are organised, make sure each group is distinct and go round each one, finding out what it is they share. If you find two groups the same ('jeans' for example) then point out that you don't want this duplication and that in the next round they must work harder to ensure that groups aren't doubled up.

Having got the idea for how it works mechanically you can then start to pose more interesting and relevant questions for them to organise around. These could be factual, like 'How long have you been at the organisation?' This gives you a very quick visual impression of the spread of experience, which is often quite surprising to people. You can also ask more conceptual questions like 'What is the biggest problem or issue you currently face?'

DEBRIEF

There isn't much debrief to this apart from identifying the groups they form in response to each question. That said, you can ask afterwards how they went about the organising, what they noticed, whether people moved much, or stayed still or developed strategies.

VARIATIONS

You can play around with the rhythm here. Either you can make the questions simple and let them find groups quickly, or pose more complex questions, play more slowly and really make sure they have proper conversations. One Associate Fellow I explained this to at Oxford used it to great effect over the course of several hours with a group from a bank.

THINGS TO WATCH OUT FOR

One of the great things about this game is that you can only be in one group. It can be really useful in forcing people to confront ambiguities. I once played with a digital media agency in New York and the response to the simple instruction 'stand in your departments' elicited nearly an hour of conversation. The highly plastic and changing nature of their business meant that it wasn't at all obvious where some of the people should be and they couldn't stand in two places. Had we only talked about it, this paradox would have been buried under lots of clever language, but making it physical flushed it out. So if you want to wheedle out something like that, this is a great game to play.

WHEN TO USE INCORPORATIONS

This is a great 'getting to know you' game. You can make the questions about personal interests or professional history but one way or another you identify people that have things in common. It's good to include the odd eccentric question, because that creates some unexpected groups.

The other great use for this is to get feedback, about the session itself or ideas that have been generated. Doing this physically forces people to take a position and makes the spectrum of opinion very tangible in the room. It also has the nice side effect of getting them out of their chairs.

———

Finally, an invitation. I hope you try these ideas out and let me know what happens. I love it when I get to observe someone I have taught games to in action, or when someone contacts me with a story about how they have used an exercise. It is beautiful to see how someone else uses a game and I always learn something. They will have changed, added or improved things in a way that I wouldn't think of. So don't be limited by what I say, don't be shy to mess around with them and don't be slow to get in touch and tell me what happened.

I am afraid we don't have any idea where we learned this one.

About the Author

Robert Poynton (www.robertpoynton.com) lives in an off-grid, solar-powered house just outside the small town of Arenas de San Pedro in the province of Avila, in rural Spain with his wife and 3 sons. From there he helps run On Your Feet, a small consultancy conveniently based in Portland, Oregon, that he co-founded with Gary Hirsch (see www.oyf.com). On Your Feet uses improvisational ideas, tools and experiences to help people in organisations work together more effectively and creatively. Much of the learning that led to this book has been gleaned from working with a wonderful array of On Your Feet clients over the past 12 years.

Robert is also an Associate Fellow of the Said Business School at Oxford University and was visiting Praxis Research Associate at Green Templeton College, Oxford, in 2010. At Oxford he works in Executive Education, primarily on leadership programmes. He is also a moderator of the Oxford Praxis Forum at Green Templeton College, a new venture designed as a collaboration between practitioners and academics to explore the future of leadership and the leadership of the future.

In addition Robert is an Associate Partner at eatbigfish, a challenger brand consultancy, with whom he has collaborated for more than 10 years, often as founder Adam Morgan's partner in games of ideas tennis.

Although he travels widely, Robert also uses the local environment in his work. He hosts Parenthesis Executive Decompression in Arenas de San Pedro. Born out of 10 years working with senior executives at Oxford, these are individual retreats personally designed for senior leaders to reflect on dilemmas or turning points in their careers. He recently ran the 'Creative Tapas Experiment' - an exploration of co-creativity, improvisation and leadership masquerading as a party. He continues to experiment with mixing creative work and reflection with physical work such as olive picking.

Thanks

Thanks to Gary Hirsch at On Your Feet for being my improv point man. To Marshall Young at Oxford University for helping me see the bigger picture. To all On Your Feet's clients and all the executives who have come to Oxford, for being bold enough to try this stuff and for giving me rich seams of feedback and confidence as a result.

To Andy Middleton for inviting me to the Do Lectures and thus unleashing this particular adventure. To Miranda West of Do Books, for her beguiling and engaging invitation to write a 'Ladybird' book and for providing incredibly valuable help, direction and feedback throughout the process, with a minimum of fuss and interference.

Thanks also to all my friends in Arenas de San Pedro who provide the most wonderfully rich, varied, stimulating company in the most unlikely of places. You give me invaluable perspective as well as endless enjoyment.

Particular thanks to my three sons Bruno, Mateo and Pablo, who are a constant source of inspiration, learning and joy on our daily and heavily improvised voyage of discovery.

But most of all, enormous, heartfelt, prodigious thanks to my wonderful wife Beatriz. She never wavered in her enthusiasm for another book, though she knew it would mean a lot of extra work for her. Even more importantly, when it got tough and I couldn't see a way out she gave me context, support, ideas and suggestions without which I never would have made it. I don't think she will ever realise quite how much of this book is down to her.

Gracias por todo, de verdad.

Index